T. K. Reilly

BEHAVE!

Etiquette Lessons for Adults

iUniverse, Inc.
Bloomington

Behave!
Etiquette Lessons for Adults

Copyright © 2011, 2012 Etiquette Lessons Foundation

All rights reserved. No part of this book may be used or reproduced by any means, graphic, electronic, or mechanical, including photocopying, recording, taping or by any information storage retrieval system without the written permission of the publisher except in the case of brief quotations embodied in critical articles and reviews.

iUniverse books may be ordered through booksellers or by contacting:

iUniverse
1663 Liberty Drive
Bloomington, IN 47403
www.iuniverse.com
1-800-Authors (1-800-288-4677)

Because of the dynamic nature of the Internet, any Web addresses or links contained in this book may have changed since publication and may no longer be valid. The views expressed in this work are solely those of the author and do not necessarily reflect the views of the publisher, and the publisher hereby disclaims any responsibility for them.

Any people depicted in stock imagery provided by Thinkstock are models, and such images are being used for illustrative purposes only.

Certain stock imagery © Thinkstock.

ISBN: 978-1-4620-6174-7 (sc)
ISBN: 978-1-4620-6175-4 (e)

Printed in the United States of America

iUniverse rev. date: 12/12/2012

Dedicated
to

Sterling Character

Preface

Jack seeks help to change the way he is and in doing so, becomes an active participant in Etiquette Lessons. Behave! addresses his concerns on comportment and demeanor, protocol training, dining and drinking etiquette and conversation. Each lesson is delivered with practical activities, applied science and a test to help with cognition and retention. Behave! is guaranteed to help adults learn skills and techniques that replace nervousness with confidence by learning conduct, table manners and social protocol for adults. These lessons apply to the broad view and prospect of social events on every adult's horizon. Social skill details learned here will prepare you for countless meetings, luncheons, breakfasts, five and seven - course banquets, cocktail parties or dinners you must attend throughout your career. Here you will acquire knowledge of what to wear, what to do, what to expect, even what to say.

Featured as a demonstration in protocol and dining etiquette, Lesson Twelve is a three-act play titled, "Moon Lake." Set in a conference room and a high-end dining room, "Moon Lake," is a dramatization of three important, meetings between two teams of business executives. Every lesson Jack has learned throughout the book is used in "Moon Lake." To make this final lesson more timely and interesting; because the world grows smaller each day and professional skills might include the added dimension of multi-cultural etiquette, the executives in Lesson Twelve present Western and Eastern cultures meeting in Singapore. "Moon Lake," can be read or acted out on stage.

Acknowledgements

Etiquette Lessons instructional training system began at home and has gone global. Over the past decade I have taught thousands of students, packed seminars and filled two books of lessons. High demand for Etiquette Lessons prompted an online instructor certification program that has trained and certified hundreds of etiquette instructors now teaching Etiquette Lessons in their own small businesses nationwide and abroad. Until now Etiquette Lessons were written for youth. I am very happy to present my third book, 'Behave! Etiquette Lessons for Adults.' Not only will it serve individuals as a self-help book, it will expand the etiquette instructors' client base and help them fill the need for civility in modern society from the top down with etiquette classes for adults. Many thanks to the instructors for endorsing and using my curriculum. I applaud their professionalism, enthusiasm and results!

One April night, the motivation to write the lessons for adults arrived from Manhattan in an e-mail. It came via request link to customer service on my web site: www.etiquettelessons.com. To protect the privacy of the person who sent the request, I have changed his name to Jack. Jack's e-mail is reprinted at the beginning of Lesson One. Behave! Etiquette Lessons for Adults, contains all the lessons he needs to know. Written with Jack in mind, these lessons are for adults who puzzle over positive self-representation, mastery of self-image, drinking and dining skills (especially knife-and-fork skills) and conversation skills. Jack and many adults like him will find missing pieces to their own puzzle in Behave! Thanks to him.

Finally, to my advisors on business abroad and foreign affairs protocol, Kevin and Kojak, Thank you for nudging me out of naivety and bringing me up to speed on how actual, international negotiations are conducted in Singapore. I believe your input will guide Etiquette Lessons readers to the paths you found. Thank you, Merci, Gracias, Danke, Grazie, Spasibo, Obrigado, Xie xie ni, Arigato!

Content

Preface vii
Acknowledgements ix
Introduction xiii
Lesson 1. Inspiration 1
Lesson 2. Comportment 7
Lesson 3. Protocol 13
Lesson 4. Personal Check List 17
Lesson 5. Personal Code of Conduct 21
Lesson 6. Conversation 29
Lesson 7. Correspondence 35
Lesson 8. Dining Etiquette 41
Lesson 9. The Concert Style of Dining . . . 47
Lesson 10. Connoisseur 51
Lesson 11. Formal Attire 63
Lesson 12. Moon Lake 67
Sources 85
Author Biography 87

Introduction

Etiquette training enables us to remain aloof as we interact with others. Etiquette guides us from behind the scenes. Etiquette's luxurious veneer of civility delivers appropriate behavior while simultaneously, allowing our brains to memorize, evaluate and think ahead. A working knowledge of Protocol, the rules of meeting, helps us navigate toward goals as we select allies, meet the competition and network forward. Etiquette and protocol are two essential investments for building an overall image. Like the pedals of a bicycle, etiquette and protocol are social skills and good manners that get us where we are going.

Knowing how to behave empowers you to go forward in pursuit of success and good fortune. Invest yourself fully in etiquette training; leave bad habits and bad attitudes, bad company and above all, bad language at the gate. You are about to embrace a new overall image and represent yourself in a more positive, ethical way. A way that brings with it what is known as 'loving what you do.' Plus, through the far reaching, positive effects of your actions, by planting seeds of civility along the road to success you will 'give back' much more than you take.

Take a moment to breathe deeply and feel the rhythm of your own heart. This fragile life is your true possession. Protect it with diligence and self-control. Good health provides a long view and a realistic measure of your influence. Etiquette Lessons training requires high levels of awareness, fitness and commitment from adults because good behavior is not just part of your life, it is your legacy.

Lesson One

INSPIRATION

"I AM LOOKING for help in my overall image and professional dining skills. I have been told that I have issues with the way I hold my fork and I tend to drink a lot when I am around clients or am nervous. I have been unemployed for a year and know that the way I am needs to change as I am not able to represent myself in a positive way."

Hello, Who's this at my garden gate?

My name is Jack, I wrote to you last night, I am looking for help.

Hi, Please call me T.K. You sent the e-mail from Manhattan? Well, it came to the right place. We've already custom designed the Etiquette Lessons you requested. I see you brought a friend. Is this the person who commented on how you hold a fork?

Yes, Sorry I didn't introduce you. This is my sister, Jill. She is always talking about etiquette. What is this place?

I'm happy to meet you too, Jill. You could become an etiquette instructor.

I hope so, that's why I'm here..

This place is my Garden of Inspiration, Jack.

Your e-mail inspired me to write, Behave! Etiquette Lessons for Adults. I've had many requests for this book in the past, but the sense of urgency in your e-mail is a real call to action. Now that you are here, we can begin to address your issues. You are the central figure in the presentation of twelve etiquette lessons.

Great, Thank you! When do we get started?

Right now, Please walk with me, this path leads to the shores of Moon Lake. Your lessons in table manners, conversation, drinking, dining, attire, everything in your e-mail will be presented along the way. To establish a frame of reference, I will start with an historical review:

About thirty-two thousand years ago, human tribes began to populate every continent of the Earth. Ancients developed dwellings near rivers, fertile land, sea ports and crossroads. They learned to fish, farm, sail and produce crops. They developed language, art, spiritual rituals; invented hunting and building tools and weaponry for protection and conquest. They used mathematics to build monuments of stone: In 2560 BCE (*Before Common Era*) Egypt, the Great Pyramid of Giza was built and in England, 2400 - 2200 BCE, Stonehenge. Construction of China's Great Wall began in 200 BCE and continued up to 1644 CE (Common Era). Inca pyramids were built in South America in 200 BCE. In pre-Hispanic Mexico, Mayan and Aztec pyramids were built 300 - 1200 CE.

Will there be a test after this? Heh heh.

Yes, of course. Each lesson ends with a quiz, a writing assignment or some memorization to aid retention and cognition. Please stay on the path.

After the Stone Age, real expansion began. Using celestial navigation and the compass, Viking ships sailed to North America, 750 - 1050 CE. By the late Middle Ages and through the Renaissance, 1350 - 1600 CE, European explorers and merchant ships ventured onto the open seas. The sextant was invented in the 17th century, improving navigation. Commerce was established among the merchant class, European royalty, clergy, natives and colonists. Exploration brought European immigration, civilization and culture to the Americas. Any questions?

Yes, When did the pilgrims arrive?

The pilgrims arrived at Plymouth, Massachusetts in 1621.

Who are these marble statues of?

The four statues ahead are a tribute to the masters of etiquette, represented here in the Roman style of sculpture, wearing togas and carrying iconic symbols. Each master of etiquette set the standard of social conduct for their time. They modernized rules set forth by their predecessors. Their lives and works are milestones in the evolution of etiquette.

The first statue is of Catherine de Medici, ruler of France, 1547- 59. She implemented the use of dining utensils at French court dinners during the late Renaissance by providing her guests with innovative, two-tined Italian forks to carry bites of food from the table to the mouth. Before then, Europeans ate with knives, spoons and their fingers. In some Eastern cultures, India and Arabia, for example, people traditionally eat with their fingers while in most of Asia, chopsticks are used. Catherine de Medici's statue holds the knife fork and spoon used in Western style dining.

During the sixteenth century, refined manners known as *etiquette* became popular with royalty in France, Italy and England. The word *etiquette* was derived from the name of a special card, ticket or ribbon that was used as an invitation allowing admittance to royal court events.

A will to conform still proceeds opportunity for advancement among civilized people. People relax when those around them behave in a predictable manner. When a group's rules of protocol and etiquette are observed, each member is allowed in turn the opportunity to attract or charm and entertain others. This behavior applies no matter who the leaders of a particular group may be. Most newcomers simply attend and gradually advance, earning social status. Some are born into their social position and must work to keep it. A few inspire innovations that alter tradition. Some members of society make sweeping changes to the good or the bad. Thankfully it is the nature of society to balance itself.

The second statue in my Garden of Inspiration is George Washington, first US President, 1789 - 97. Washington's, *Rules of Civility*, (courtesy) reprinted in lesson three, set the standard for himself as boy and man and for the officers of the Continental Army under his command. His code of conduct remains in the public domain as steadfast fatherly advice for all gentlemen and ladies today. The sword his statue carries is a symbol of leadership and duty. (http://www.donnayoung.org/penmanship/gw-notebook.htm)

Eighteenth-century revolutions turned the tables in France and England. Ideas became the property of the people…including etiquette and political protocol. In France, Liberty from ruling monarchs brought everyman freedom and sovereignty. In America this began with the Continental Congress, the Declaration of Independence, the Constitution of the United States, the Bill of Rights and the Emancipation Proclamation. In each American's heart of hearts, virtually every man is king in his own castle. Every woman is queen in hers. All girls are Princesses, boys are Prince Charming.

Early Americans practiced European traditions of fine dining and social grace. New styles were imported with newcomers or added out of necessity. Pioneers moved westward setting tables across the nation with heirloom linens, tableware and prayer books they had packed in trunks. Ladies and gentlemen in government, military, education, religion and all professions socialized at countless gatherings both casual and formal establishing strong national social support systems and infrastructure.

The third statue is of course, Queen Victoria, monarch of the UK, 1837 - 1901. She reigned for 63 years. During that time, America had 17 different elected presidents. The 'Victorian' era brought industry, education and etiquette to middle class society. Victoria's reign is defined by strict standards of personal morality and rigid rules of social etiquette. Her influence spread throughout the British Empire, structuring middle class life by association, worldwide. Her statue holds a small replica of the Earth. (http//vicorianstation.com)

Nineteenth and twentieth century American culture emanated from centers of industry and government. From New England came propriety, decorum, and the arts, confidence from the sheer power and magnetism of New York and legendary pride and hospitality of the South. A successful, two-party system of government, developed electing dynamic leaders with term limitations. Moving west, we added bold business in oil and cattle, automobiles, the gold rush in California, railroads, electricity, telephones and National Parks. This was the era of Theodore Roosevelt, America's 26th president from 1901 -1909.

The fourth statue represents American author, Emily Post, 1872 - 1960. In 1922, She published a book of tips on conduct titled, *Etiquette in Society, in Business, in Politics and at Home*. Her career began during the end of the Victorian Era and spanned history from the stock-market crash of 1929, the Great Depression, which lasted until 1941 when America entered World War II, the Cold War in 1945, and the launch of Sputnik in 1957. Her statue is holding her book. (http://www.victoriastation.com)

America bounced back from depression and war in the Pacific and Europe and the latter half of the twentieth-century brought technological advances, industry and immigration, Hollywood with powerful imagery of glamour and sports to entertain us, airplanes for transport, freeway systems, the annexation of Hawaii and Alaska, Income Tax and Social Security, television with new lifestyle imagery and advertising, space travel, plastics, communication satellites, computers, newcomers from Asia, Mexico and the Near East, higher education for the masses, longer life-span through modern medicine, increased foreign trade and foreign affairs, the internet and Homeland Defense.

The twenty-first is a hungry new century growing through pains of economic and political change; searching for safe paths to the future. Now the world population is electronically connected. Communication is the world's partner in the existence of Democracy. Many generations have brought civilized culture to this point. Ethnic strands from around the world, weave daily into a grand, global tablecloth. The central point in the home is a table where food is served with a good deal of tradition behind it.

Lesson One - Inspiration - Lesson Activity - Bookwalk

Well, there you have it, a history of the evolution of etiquette, a foundation to build upon. Before we continue, it is time for the activity that goes with this lesson, the *Bookwalk*. Quite simply, I want you to place this book on your head and walk while keeping your body straight yet relaxed—not stiff.

(Not recommended for Ebooks.) With a book atop your head. Walk out and back about eight paces each way turning slowly to keep the book in place before your return. The *Bookwalk* gives balance to your gait, promotes good posture and the dignified point of view of an upstanding man or woman. As you know, modern humans belong to the primate species, *homo sapiens*. As such, one of our defining characteristics is that we are bipedal, we walk on two legs. (Plato once defined man as a featherless biped.) In the interest of good self-representation, learn to walk well, carry yourself well. Walk steadily with smooth, confident motion forward, shoulders back, abs taut, with your ribcage held up. Hold your chin slightly upward and point your nose where you are looking. Work on that. (http://humanorigins.si.edu/evidence/human-fossils/species/homo-sapiens)

Excuse me, TK, Looking ahead, I see signs posted. What are they?

Those are excerpts or 'call outs' from Etiquette Lessons, they are actually the *signs* of good etiquette that will manifest in your behavior once you learn these lessons.

Time for the quiz. Have a seat. Here's a pen. It's an open book exam and the answer key is in the back of the book. Good luck to both of you!

Lesson One, Inspiration - Quiz

1. Humans began to populate Earth_____ years ago.

2. Stone Age monuments still standing in Africa, England, China, Mexico and South America were built using _____.

3. Early sailors used celestial navigation, the compass and later, the sextant to navigate the open seas. What is used today?_____

4. When did the Pilgrims arrive at Plymouth, MA? _____

5. What are the world's three ways of lifting bites of food from table to the mouth? _____

6. What is the meaning of civility?_____

7. Name three documents that guarantee America's democracy. _____
_____

8. When was Queen Victoria's reign?_____

9. Which American president established the National Parks System? _____
_____

10. What started the Great Depression of 1929 and when did it end? _____
_____

Lesson Two
COMPORTMENT

This lesson is a lecture so you may as well remain seated until the activity at the end. You might want to take notes.

Comport, a transitive verb meaning, *to behave*. This old term enters our discourse to deliver a directive for today's generation of young adults. Comport! From Latin: *comportare* to bring together, to carry. First known use: 1589, Synonyms: accord, agree, answer, chord, cohere, coincide, check, conform, consist, correspond, dovetail, fit, go, harmonize, jibe, rhyme, sort, square, tally.

Be in accord with reasonable and acceptable standards and policies as expressed in the myriad of immediate and long range choices you make regarding how you carry yourself when you walk, your clothing, language, conduct and behavior.

"Comport yourself with dignity and grace."

When playing the host at large, take care to choose venues with a reputation for successful business and social events. The menu, furniture, view and service in a dining establishment can make or break the success of plans. Give every presentation your best effort. Guests will appreciate the effort and reciprocate in kind. You will feel respected and look forward to future meetings. In business, initial presentations set the standard for follow ups with sales support, customer service and even product development.

At business meetings, people talk, listen and make decisions soberly during business hours. In meetings, agreements can be formalized, finalized and documented, recorded and followed-up with on the same day. Networking will inevitably bring you to choices of business and social organizations of which you would like to become a member. Membership may come with college affiliation, fraternity or sorority, job or profession or you may be invited and sponsored in joining a professional association, society or organization

Become familiar with a little book called, "Robert's Rules of Order." This will teach you how any organization's business meetings are conducted. (Who can vote and how to make a 'motion', etc). A working understanding of these procedures is essential if you wish to sit on any executive board of directors, especially if you aspire to become an officer or director. Good standing in one or more professional or charitable organizations can certainly help build your overall image while providing you a broader view with valuable introductions and opportunities galore. (http:www.rulesonline.com)

"Aim to Please."

Presentations, negotiations, interviews and club meetings often take place at executive lunches; while dinners are generally reserved for celebrations, entertainment, recreation, socializing, fine wines, romance and relaxation. If you are hosting, where will you plan to meet? One good way to get hosting help is to be a social member in a private club with good dining and conference facilities. If you travel to business meetings perhaps your company is a member of an upscale hotel chain or patronizes an upscale restaurant chain where service and food are consistently good. You get consistently good service when the head waiter knows you personally, you have a favorite table, where perhaps the menus show no prices to guests and you can run a tab and pay monthly fees. You want the meetings to be in a place where you know what to expect so that you can relax and focus on business. Yacht clubs, riding clubs, athletic clubs, golf and country clubs have social memberships expressly for the use of such dining facilities. You may need to be sponsored by a member and pay a fee to join but you will find that this level of comfort is designed for and by successful business people. These venues have good parking, valets, meeting and banquet rooms with audio/visual aids and telephone conferencing, well-trained waiters and service staff. Some even employ restroom attendants who can sew on a button, clean-off a food spill, clean or replace a gentleman's neck tie, repair a lady's broken nail or maybe even a broken heel or replace snagged tights. Private clubs and fine venue restrooms provide cologne, deodorant, hair spray, make-up, shoe polish, and such to help you and your guest keep the edge on your professional image. Naturally, you will arrive at the venue looking your best by keeping and following a personal standard.

Regarding placement of hands at the table, customs vary. In most countries, fellow diners like to see everyone's hands on top of the table where everyone can see them. In America, hands may be folded and in your lap or folded with wrists placed on the table edge in front of you while you are not eating. One wrist may be resting on the edge of the table for support at anytime while the other hand rests in your lap. Keep your forearms off the table, your elbows at your sides and heed the collective cry of grandmothers everywhere:

"Keep your elbows off the table."

Learning and practicing all the nuances of comportment and decorum in the world should not prevent you from expressing yourself and your free will with personality. On the contrary, etiquette knowledge fosters engineered self-expression. Personality is the icing on the cake. With etiquette training, you should feel more yourself than ever because you will have learned to comport yourself with grace and dignity and have the assurance others should not be offended by your behavior. If you still need to understand your own nature as regards the ways in which you do things, objective knowledge about your individual personality type helps. It definitely makes sense to take a free, informal personality test online. In fact, the results will enhance your resume. Plus the results will help you choose which career path is right for you. Are you a self starter, a leader, a follower or an observer? Knowing the signs of personality types can help you identify personality types of others and discover how to work best with them. The best way to understand personalities or psychological types is to take one of many personality tests like the MBTI® (Myers Briggs Type Indicator) instrument.

"Play to the Strengths in Your Personality."

Easily accessed on the web, this information will help you to understand who you are as others see and hear you, and you can learn to make the most of your strengths. You will learn to identify traits in others as well. This will also help you to adapt the way you naturally do things or how you have learned to do things, to truly proper and polite ways of etiquette and protocol. (Hopefully this will only require a few adjustments.) We each have refinements to make. I have learned to modulate my voice, for example, but still, I definitely need a microphone for public speaking. Thankfully writing is one of my strengths, so the power of publishing is taking my books of Etiquette Lessons much farther than my speaking voice ever could.

Social Media

Memberships, associations, personality test results and well-written resumes all enhance your ability to impress prospective employers, clients and friends. But make no mistake, they will also check your online presence to get a more complete picture of you. It is important to create a professional networking profile to boost your credibility. Recommendations will go before you like a personal introduction to prospective employers, clients, family and friends. Ask previous employers, professors and colleagues to post references for you on a professional network like Linkedin or Xing, for example. Meanwhile, let your personal, online presence, on: Facebook, Twitter, Myspace, YouTube, Skype, Tumblr, other blogging and podcast sites serve to compliment your image or brand with non-controversial, wholesome content. Keep your online presence dignified and professional, if it isn't, clean it up!

"Good Posture is a sign of Good Etiquette."

Stand, walk and sit up straight! Good Posture is always important. In fact it is a big sign of good etiquette and good manners. It shows that you are fit, alert, respectful, healthy, well rested and agile. Good Posture is an example to show that traditions are usually based in scientific truth or logic. If everyone sits up straight, their stomach and lungs will have plenty of room to function during the full course of a meal. Your companions will get a positive impression of you and will tend to straighten their posture as well. Also, your clothes will look best if your frame is as straight as can be. Remember the *Bookwalk* in Lesson One and please keep your rib cage held up, your shoulders back and relaxed, abs taut.

" Victorian Era, Lord Chesterfield, in his letters to his son, says 'Dancing is in itself a very trifling and silly thing but it is one of those established follies to which people of sense are sometimes obliged to conform; and then they should be able to do it well. And though I would not have you a dancer, yet, when you do dance, I would have you dance well, as I would have you do everything you do well.' In another letter he writes, 'Do you mind your dancing while your dancing master is with you? As you will be often under the necessity of dancing a minuet. I would have you dance it very well. Remember that the graceful motion of the arms, the giving of your hand and the putting off and putting on of your hat genteelly, are the material parts of a gentleman's dancing. But the greatest advantage of dancing well is, that it necessarily teaches you to present yourself, to sit, stand, and walk genteelly; all of which are of real importance to a man of fashion.'
(http://www.burrows.com/other/manners.html)

When applied to the present, Lord Chesterfield's advice still holds true

Behave!

today. I'm sure you will agree that physical education helps us to move well through our own space and move comfortably in groups. A working knowledge of dance floor etiquette adds a dimension of confidence and charm to your demeanor.

I think I understand what Lord Chesterfield meant and the Bookwalk was helpful too. I'm ready to learn more.

Great, you'll like the next exercise, good thing you brought Jill.

Lesson Two, Comportment - Lesson Activity - Dance Walk

For this exercise, we'll move into an open area. First you will practice walking together, then we'll introduce the ballroom dance holding position and practice walking to music. Stand face to face, please. Hands at your sides.

In ballroom dance, the lady always starts backward with her right foot, the gentleman starts forward with his left. Jill, I want you to walk backward, alone eight steps starting on your right foot. Now, Jack, walk forward eight steps toward her starting on your left foot. Add a slight spring to your step. Now Jack, walk backward eight steps away from Jill, starting on your right foot. Jill, walk eight steps toward Jack starting forward on your left foot. This time relax more. Swing your arms gracefully. Slightly pick up your heels as you walk. Tilt your face up and smile. Now we are back where we started. Do it again, but this time walk out and back together with Jill going backward and Jack walking forward, not touching each other. He begins with his left foot, she with her right. Go.

Now you are ready for the holding position. The gentleman offers the lady his left hand. She puts her right hand in it. She then puts her left hand on his right shoulder, looks into his eyes, smiles and then looks over his right shoulder. She is the couple's rear-view mirror. He puts his right hand on her back below her left shoulder blade, glances ahead, ready to lead. When the music begins, he will step forward with his left foot as she steps back with her right and then he steps forward with his right as she steps back with her left. Proceed like this together for eight steps and then reverse for eight steps. You move together on the dance floor as in a mirror image. This is the basic ballroom holding position or frame. Fix your gaze above the horizon and your countenance pleasant.

He leads a dance by sending silent signals with his right hand. More specifically, he leads by applying gentle pressure to the lady's back. With his palm he indicates, "Step backward or to the right," and with his fingertips he says, "Move to the left or step forward." With his left hand, he lifts her arm occasionally and guides her with his right hand into a twirl, dip or a swing maneuver.

Now I have no excuse to think that I don't know how to lead. This will require more practice and a partner who will let me lead, no offense—Sis.

With lessons to learn different steps and lots of practice, anyone can dance. First, try walking together backward and forward eight steps while in the holding position, listen to the music. Remember to smile. Add turns and new steps as you learn them. If you would like more basic waltz, tango, swing and cha cha dance instructions, order the Etiquette Lessons Ballroom Dance, Music CD at: www.etiquettelessons.com

"Fix your gaze above the horizon and your countenance pleasant."

Lesson Two - Comportment - Quiz

1. What does the word: comport, mean? _____.
2. What book outlines how business meetings must be conducted? _____ _____.
3. One good way to get hosting help is to join a_____.
4. Name three ways that personality tests are helpful. _____ _____.
5. Make no mistake, employers, clients, family and friends check your _____.
6. Good Posture is _____. If everyone sits up straight, our stomach and lungs will have plenty of room to function.
7. In ballroom dance, she always starts on her_____.
8. In ballroom dance, he always starts on his _____.
9. While dancing in the ballroom dance holding position or "frame," who has the rear view? _____.
10. How does he lead the dance? _____ _____.

Lesson Three

PROTOCOL

Lesson Activity note: From now on we will begin and end each lesson with appropriate salutations and farewells, firm handshakes and eye contact.

Hello again, welcome back, Jack and Jill. How are you doing?

Doing great, learning allot, thank you. What's next?

What we just did…meeting and exchanging information. This lesson is on Protocol, meaning: the rules of meeting. We all know the familiar sound of fax tones over a phone line. These are of course, audible computer protocol to send and receive a fax. Those audible codes are very similar to the physical code of behavior exchanged by humans when meeting. The Handshake, Curtsey, air-kiss, Hug and the Bow are signs of good etiquette. These familiar actions help to establish trust when meeting other individuals or when we are presented to a group. Introductions and presentations are extremely important ways of recognizing and advancing the individual. Advancing individuals increases everyone's social and business resources and in turn, advances society on the whole. When presented to an audience, ladies curtsey and gentlemen bow, when a dance is finished, ladies curtsey and gentlemen bow respectively. At formal receptions, you may be required to stand in a reception line where one group will pass before another as they shake hands, say hello and ladies might curtsey.

"The Handshake, the Curtsey, the Air-kiss, Hug and the Bow are signs of Good Etiquette."

When we meet someone in America, England and most English speaking countries, we must be prepared to shake hands, giving eye-contact. When meeting others in Asia, add a slight bow, from the waist with hands At your sides as in China or Japan, held upward with palms pressed together in a Namaste greeting, or at least a quick nod with eyes lowered. In Europe, especially France, Italy and Russia, protocol can includes a hug and air kisses or a firm grasp of your shoulders and a kiss on each cheek. French men may take a lady's hand and kiss it. Though foreign customs may take you by surprise, it would be impolite to register shock, displeasure or expectations.

When we meet someone new, of course it is customary to exchange names. In polite society everyone uses a title before his or her surname. On formal occasions even children are addressed using Miss and Mister. Titles acknowledge an adult's age and accomplishments. Titles can also help define who we are by what our job is, while at the same time protecting our privacy. There are royal titles in some cultures but not in America. Armed services personnel have military titles or ranks. Leaders of religious faiths use titles. Common titles, not gender specific, include: Captain, Chef, Dean, Doctor, Senator, President, Officer, Nurse, Principal, Sergeant, Reverend, Judge, etc. Titles are used in every country and culture.

"Proper Introductions are signs of Good Etiquette."

A gentleman is addressed as "Mr." plus his surname or as, "Sir." A lady with a wedding ring is called, "Mrs.," plus her surname, or if she is an elder lady who's name you do not know, Madam or M'am. Girls and young ladies or ladies without a wedding ring are "Miss" or "Ms." (pronounced Miz.) plus their surname. In polite society, only family and close friends use first names, nicknames or family titles, like "Dad." The first step in making and keeping new friends and impressing business associates is:

"Remember titles and names."

Here are some tips on memorization. It is a scientific fact that everyone has two types of memory: Short Term Memory (STM), which lasts only about 20 seconds, and Long Term Memory (LTM), which may last a life time. You can help yourself remember new information like names by associating them with easy to recall things already stored in your long-term memory. For example, to remember a new name, picture a fruit or vegetable or an animal the name of which begins with the same letter as a clue to the name of the person. Later, when you want to remember the name, think of the visual link and the name should come back to you. This is a visual *embedding* technique to help you commit things to long-term memory. Some people have a photographic memory and can 'take a mental picture' to review later while the rest of us must rely on visual and audio clues.

Audio imbedding helps as well. Say the person's name aloud in a sentence or two in conversation right after you meet them. Introduce them to someone else and say their name a third time. Write their name along with first impression notes or take a picture and put their name in the caption, if possible for a visual link. When you part, say their name once more.

Exchanging business cards is great for collecting name and address data and a classic way of holding a person's name in external memory. The texture, smooth or rough, of a business card can also ensure a tactile memory link. embossed letters are memorable too. When you meet someone again, particularly if you have only met once before, It is very impressive and complimentary to step up, greet them and say their title and name and introduce them to someone new. (However, data bases and business cards are only a substitute for actual recall. Let's not get too lazy about research and recall.) There is nothing quite as personal as one's name and there is no substitute for a smiling, friendly, personal greeting and personal introduction.

Lesson Three - Protocol - Activity - Virtual Reunion

This activity incorporates practice making introductions with memorization of names for quick recall. For best results, we would have a group around a table but it also works for individuals as a mental exercise in a virtual dining room. First, read the following instructions and then sit back, close your eyes and imagine eight people sitting around a dining table. These are people you know well enough to know their middle names. They are probably your closest family members, including you. Now, as host, I would ask you each in turn to introduce yourselves using your middle name only. Next, I would ask for another round of introductions; this time each person would introduce the person to his or her right and then the person to his or her left and lastly, introduce him or herself. We use family members for this exercise because it is easy to picture their faces but the middle names may be difficult to recall, giving us a reasonable, virtual 'meet and greet' experience, as well as a stress-free family reunion.

Lesson Three - Protocol - Quiz

1. What is the meaning of the term, Protocol? _____.
2. What physical actions of protocol are exchanged at meetings? _____ _____.

3. An elder lady whom you do not know would be addressed as, _____
_____.

4. The first step in making and keeping new friends is _____
_____.

5. Name the two types of memory and tell how long they can last. _____
_____.

6. Describe a visual *embedding* technique for committing names to long-term memory. _____
___ _____.

7. Give three examples of audio imbedding a name. _____
_____.

8. What can be done to enhance business cards for memory jogging? _____
_____.

9. How can a person's name be linked with additional information? _____
_____.

10. Give four examples of external memory. _____
_____.

Lesson Four
Personal Check List

Hi Jack, welcome back, where's Jill?

She'll be here soon. She called and asked me to apologize, said she is running late because she couldn't find anything to wear.

Maybe today's lesson will help prevent that sort of thing from happening.

In business meetings, be 100% Business-Minded. This means that you present yourself at your personal, professional best. Best dressed, be at your most polite, most charming, well-prepared and intelligent best. During sales presentations, prospective buyers watch for clues to personal hygiene, grooming and readiness, This is human nature of course, employers and associates do the same. Be prepared to impress or at least do not disappoint in this critical area. For example, one of the most annoying personal habits can be wearing too much fragrance. Don't send the wrong message with an overpowering scent or spoil a more sensitive person's appetite.

Always carry business cards and always remember that even a business lunch is a business transaction. Punctuate meetings with small gestures of kindness like opening the door for others and asking for items on the table rather than reaching across or in front of others. Mind your manners and don't send mixed-signals because they imply you don't mean business.

"Make a Good First Impression."

Here are some personal deportment tips and a list of obvious no-no's to keep in mind: No coughing, sneezing, scratching or open wounds, keep nose and ear hair and eyebrows trimmed, no muddy shoes, no 'bling', no visible tattoos, tight or revealing clothing, no baseball caps, no sunglasses, no portable coffee cups, no cell phone conversations, no texting, check mobile devices at prearranged intervals, no cursing, no chewing gum or "dip" (chewing tobacco) and no smoking. How are your penmanship and calculator skills? See that you think about and visualize or practice actions you might make during lunch so that you are prepared to give a professional impression. When you go out the door each morning, you should be ready to show the world who you are and what you can do. Use the following daily personal checklist as a lifelong reminder and regimen. Bear in mind that the competition has their own list of standards and they never forget it.

Hello Jill, you are just in time for the best part of this lesson. I think this will help you get organized in the mornings.

Personal Checklist

Jill
1.) Updated hair style
2.) Business makeup
3.) Clean, good quality shoes
4.) Cash, credit & ID
5.) Manicure/Pedicure
6.) Sparkling white teeth
7.) Clean, suit or skirt and blouse
8.) Education & Fitness
9.) Companion media, pen
10.) Tissues, hand sanitizer

Jack
1.) Clean-shaven or groomed face
2.) Updated haircut
3.) Clean, short fingernails
4.) Clean, quality street shoes
5.) Sparkling, white teeth
6.) Cash, credit & ID
7.) Clean suit, shirt and tie
8.) Companion media, pen
9.) Education & Fitness
10.) Tissues, handkerchief

Lesson Activity:

Seek a professional, personal make over, talk to an image consultant or personal fitness coach in person or look in top magazines, to define your ideal diet, work out, wardrobe and hair style. Purchase the best salon services and clothing you can afford.

I always rely on Sis for all that.

I know, Jack and no offense meant to you, Jill. But, this is an area where the individual has to develop his or her own taste to match requirements of stated goals and to suit their own personality. Nurture an uncompromising attitude toward self-discipline in these matters.

Lesson Four Quiz
Personal Check List

The next page is blank, use it to write the top ten items in your personal regimen and check list.

Lesson Five

PERSONAL CODE OF CONDUCT

I'M SO PROUD to present this voice from the past. Rules of Civility, written by George Washington. These personal tips on self-discipline in hygiene, grooming, voice, manners, habits and timing can help you with being considerate to others in all manner of social interactions and help ensure that your conduct will be welcome in good company. These notes in the original early American dialect make up perhaps the best portrait we have of the man who became America's first President and a national treasure.

Maybe he was trying to improve himself like I am.

Yes, of course, I'm sure he was.

> *"Labor to keep alive in your hearts that little celestial fire called conscience."* George Washington

George Washington's 18th century Rules of Civility (also known as Rules of Conduct or Rules of Decent Behavior) came to my attention in a school where I saw them being used for penmanship practice. It has been said that George Washington wrote these instructions for his officers to follow. Even in the old English, these rules speak to us now. I am reprinting this fatherly advice from the 1770's here, in Etiquette Lessons for Adults because, surely these rules can help forge sterling character in the 21st century.

George Washington's Rules of Civility

Every action done in company ought to be with some sign of respect to those who are present.

When in company, put not your hands to any part of the body, not usually discovered.

Show nothing to your friend that might affright him.

In the presence of others sing not to yourself with a humming voice nor drum with your fingers or feet.

If you cough, sneeze, sigh, or yawn, do it not loud but privately; and speak not in your yawning. Put your handkerchief or hand before your face and turn aside.

Speak not when others speak, sit not when others stand, speak not when you should hold your peace, walk not when others stop.

Put not off your clothes in the presence of others, nor go out of your chamber half dressed.

At play and at fire it is good manners to give place to the last comer and affect not speak louder than what is ordinary.

Spit not on the fire, nor stoop low before it. Neither put your hands into the flames to warm them nor set your feet upon the fire, especially if there is meat before it.

When you sit down keep your feet firm and even without putting one on the other nor crossing them.

Shift not yourself in the sight of others nor gnaw your nails.

Shake not the head, feet, or legs, roll not the eyes, lift not one eyebrow higher than the other, wry not the mouth, and bedew no man's face with your spittle by approaching too near him when you speak.

Kill no vermin as fleas, lice, ticks in the sight of others. If you see any filth or thick spittle, put your foot dexterously upon it; if it be upon the clothes of your companions, put it off privately; and if it be upon your own clothes, return thanks to him who puts it off.

Turn not your back to others especially in speaking; jog not the table or desk on which another reads or writes; lean not upon anyone.

Keep your nails clean and short, also your hands and teeth clean, yet without showing any great concern for them.

Do not puff up the cheeks, loll not out the tongue, rub the hands, or beard, trust out the lips, or bite them, keep the lips too open or close.

Be no flatterer, neither play with any that delights not to be played with.

Read no letters, books, or papers in company; but when there is a necessity for the doing of it, you must ask leave. Come not near the books or writings of another so as to read them or give your opinion of them unasked; also look not nigh when another is writing a letter.

Let your countenance be pleasant, but in serious matters somewhat grave.

The gestures of the body must be suited to the discourse your are upon.

Reproach none for the infirmities of nature, nor delight to put them that have in mind of thereof.

Show not yourself glad at the misfortune of another, though he were your enemy.

When you see a crime punished, you may be inwardly pleased, but always show pity to the suffering offender.

Do not laugh too much or too loud in public.

Superfluous compliments and all affectation of ceremony are to be avoided, yet where due, they are not to be neglected.

In pulling off your hat to persons of distinction, as noblemen, justices, churchmen, etc., make a reverence, bowing more or less according to the custom of the better bred and quality of the person. Among your equals, expect not always that they should begin with you first, but to pull off your hat when there is no need is affectation in the matter of saluting and resulting in words, keep to the most usual custom.

'Tis ill manners to bid one more eminent than yourself be covered as well as not to do it to whom it is due; likewise, he that makes too much haste to put on his hat does not well, yet he ought to put it on at the first, or at most the second time of being asked. Now what is herein spoken, of qualification in behavior or saluting ought to be observed in taking of place, and sitting down for ceremonies without bounds is troublesome.

If anyone comes to speak with you while you are sitting, stand up, though he be your inferior; and when you present seats, let it be to everyone according to his degree.

When you meet with one of greater quality than yourself, stop and retire, especially if it be a door to give way for him to pass.

In walking the highest place in most countries seems to be on the hand, therefore, place yourself on the left of him whom you desire to honor; but if three walk together, the mid place is the most honorable, the wall is usually given to the most worthy if two walk together.

To one that is your equal, or not much inferior, you are to give the chief place in your lodging; and he to whom it is offered ought at the first to refuse it, but at the second accept it, though not without acknowledging his own unworthiness.

They that are in dignity or in office have in all places precedency; but whilst they are young, they ought to respect those that are their equals in birth or other qualities, though they have no public charge.

If anyone far surpasses others, either in age, or estate, or merit, yet would give place to one meaner than himself in his own lodging, the one ought not accept it; so he, on the other hand, should not use much earnestness or offer it above once or twice.

Let your discourse with men of business be short and comprehensive.

It is good manners to prefer them to whom we speak before ourselves, especially if they be above us with whom in no sort we ought to begin.

In visiting the sick, do not presently play the physician if you be not knowing therein.

Artificers and persons of low degree ought not to use many ceremonies to Lords or others of high degree, but respect and highly honor them; and those of high degree ought to treat them with affability and courtesy, without arrogance.

In speaking to men of quality, do not lean or look them full in the face, nor approach near them, at least keep a full pace from them.

Strive not with your superiors in argument, but always submit your judgment to others with modesty.

In writing or speaking, give every person his due title according to his degree and the custom of the place.

Do not express joy before one who is sick or in pain, for that contrary passion will aggravate his misery.

Undertake not to teach your equal in the art himself professes; it savors of arrogance.

Let thy ceremonies in courtesy be proper to the dignity of his place with whom thou converses, for it is absurd to act the same with a clown and a prince.

When a man does all he can though it succeeds not well blame not him that did it.

Mock not nor jest at anything of importance; break no jests that are sharp biting; and if you deliver anything witty and pleasant, abstain from laughing thereat yourself.

Being to advise or reprehend any one, consider whether it ought to be in public or in private, presently or at some other time, in what terms to do it; and reproving show no sign of choler, but do it with all mildness and sweetness.

Wherein you reprove another be unblameable yourself, for example is more prevalent than precepts.

Take all admonitions thankfully in what time or place given but afterwards, not being culpable, take a time and place convenient to let him know that gave it.

Use no reproachful language against any one; neither curse or revile.

Wear not your clothes foul, ripped or dusty, but see that they be brushed once every day, at least, and take heed that you approach not to any uncleanness.

Be not hasty to believe flying reports to the disparagement of any.

In your apparel be modest and endeavor to accommodate nature, rather than to procure admiration, keep to the fashion of your equals, such as are civil and orderly with respect to times and places.

Play not the peacock, looking everywhere about you, to see if you be well decked, if your shoes fit well, if your stockings sit neatly, and clothes handsomely.

Run not in the streets; neither go too slowly with your mouth open; go not shaking your arms, kick not the earth with your feet; go not upon the toes nor in a dancing fashion.

Eat not in the streets, nor in the house out of season.

Associate yourself with men of good quality, if you esteem your own reputation for it is better to be alone than in bad company.

In walking up and down in a house, only with one in company if he be greater than yourself, at the first give him the right hand and stop not till he does and be not the first that turns; and when you turn let it be with your face towards him. If he be a man of great quality, walk not with him cheek by jowl, but somewhat behind him, but yet in a manner that he may easily speak to you.

Let your conversation be without malice or envy, for it is a sign of a tractable and commendable nature; and in all cases of passion admit reason to govern.

Never express anything unbecoming nor act against the rules moral before your inferiors.

Be not immodest in urging your friends to discover a secret.

Utter not base and frivolous things amongst grave and learned men; nor very difficult questions or subjects among the ignorant; or with things hard to be believed, stuff not your discourse with sentences, amongst your betters nor equals.

Speak not of doleful things in a time of mirth or at the table; speak not of melancholy things as death and wounds, and if others mention them, change the discourse if you can. Tell not your dreams, but to your intimate friends.

A man ought not to value himself of his achievements or rare qualities of wit, much less his riches, virtue or kindred.

Break not a jest where non takes pleasure in mirth; laugh not aloud, not at all without occasion, deride no man's misfortune, though there seems to be some cause.

speak not injurious words, neither in jest not earnest; scoff at none although they give occasion.

Be not forward but friendly and courteous be the first to salute, hear, and answer, and be not pensive when it's time to converse.

Detract not from others; neither be excessive in commanding.

Go not thither, where you know not, whether you shall be welcome or not. Give not advice without being asked and when desired do it briefly.

If two contend together, take not the part of either unconstrained; and be not obstinate in your own opinion; in things indifferent be of the major side.

Reprehend not the imperfection of others, for that belongs to parents, masters, and superiors.

Gaze not on the marks or blemishes of others and ask not how they came. What you may speak in secret to your friend, deliver not to others.

Speak not in an unknown tongue in company, but in your own language and that as those of quality do an not as the vulgar. Sublime matters treat seriously.

Think before you speak; pronounce to imperfectly nor bring ut your words to hastily, but distinctly and orderly.

When another speaks be attentive yourself and disturb not the audience; if any hesitate in his words, help him not, nor prompt him without desired; interrupt him not, nor answer him till his speech be ended.

In the midst of discourse ask not of what one treateth, but of you perceive any stop because of your coming you may well entreat him gently to proceed. If a person of quality comes in while you are conversing, it is handsome to repeat what was said before.

While you are talking, point not your finger at him of whom you discourse nor approach too near him to whom you talk, especially to his face.

Treat with men at fit times abut business; and whisper not in the company of others.

Make no comparisons; and if any of the company be commended for any brave act of virtue, commend not another for the same.

Be not apt to relate news if you know not the truth thereof. In discoursing of things you have heard, name not your author; always a secret discover not.

Be not tedious in discourse or in reading unless you find the company pleased therewith.

Be not curious to know the affairs of others; neither approach those that speak in private.

Undertake not what you cannot perform, but be careful to keep your promise.

When you deliver a matte do it with passion and discretion, however mean the person be you do it to.

When your superiors talk to anybody, hearken not neither speak nor laugh.

In company of those of higher quality than yourself, speak not until you are asked a question, then stand upright, put off your hat and answer in few words.

Being set at meat, scratch not ; neither cough, spit, or blow your nose, except if there is a necessity for it.

Make a show of talking great delight in your victuals; feed not with greediness; cut your bread with a knife; lean not on the table; neither find fault with what you eat.

Entertaining anyone at the table it is decent to present him with meat.

If you soak bread in the sauce, let it be no more than what you put in your mouth at a time; and blow not your broth at the table; stay till it cools itself.

Put not another bite into your mouth till the former be swallowed. Let not your morsels be too big.

Drink not, nor talk with your mouth full, neither gaze about while you are drinking.

Drink not too leisurely, nor yet too hastily; before and after drinking, wipe your lips; breath not then or ever with too great a noise, for it is uncivil.

Cleanse not your teeth with the table cloth napkin, fork, or knife, but if others do it, let it be done with a pick tooth.

Rinse not your mouth in the presence of others.

It is out of use to call upon the company often to eat; nor need you drink to others every time you drink.

In company of your betters, be not longer in eating than they are; lay not your arm but only your hand upon the table.

It belongs to the chiefest in company to unfold his napkin and fall to meat first, but he ought then to begin in time and dispatch with dexterity that the slowest may have time allowed him.

Be not angry at table whatever happens, and if you have reason to be, show it not; put on a cheerful countenance especially if there be strangers, for good humor makes one dish of meat a feast.

Set not yourself at the upper end of the table; but if it be your due or that the master of the house would have it so, contend not, least you should trouble the company.

If others talk at the table, be attentive; but talk not with meat in your mouth.

If others speak of God or his attributes, let it be seriously and with reverence. Honor and obey your natural parents although they be poor.

Let your recreations be manful not sinful.

Labor to keep alive in your breast that little celestial fire called conscience.

Lesson Five - Personal Code of Conduct - Activity and Quiz:

On the following blank page, write an essay describing how you can apply Washington's Rules of Civility to life in your world.

Lesson Six

CONVERSATION

G'day, mates, how many different greetings do you know?

Hello, I know that was from Australia or New Zealand. I guess I know about four. But I bet after this lesson, I will know more, right?

Yes! But whichever language you choose to speak, make sure you have something to say. Be prepared with something for small talk. No one likes a know-it-all, but everyone likes their associates to be well informed. Read daily news headlines. Know current affairs, important sports scores and weather forecasts. Know the names of the top ten people in power in the world, in your field and in your company. Always have the answer if someone asks or say, "I don't know but I can find out." There are many search engines standing by to help you find those answers. After dinner parties, your most often used compliment should be, "The food was delicious," (directed to host and hostess.) Speaking of whom, when you are invited to dinner be sure to bring a 'hostess gift,' a small gift such as a bouquet of flowers or box of candy for the hostess. In conversation, your jokes should be harmless, ice breakers like, " What do you get when you cross a centipede with a parrot?...............a Walkie Talkie!" Longer, complicated jokes and riddles require practice to get the punch line right. If you sense a lull in the conversation and decide to tell a story, be sure that you know what you are talking about and how to bring the story to a close or answer related questions.

Be attentive to other's interests. Ask questions. Encourage others to talk about themselves. Dinner conversation for example, should flow from one person to the other in a continuous fashion, occasionally punctuated with mirth. Think before you speak. Be aware that you are opening, carrying, listening to, or redirecting dinner conversation. Conversation is something like a babbling brook, game of cards, a ball game or a board game. It keeps moving and everyone takes a turn or passes. Listen closely to others. It's a well-known fact that a charming person is one who is a good listener. Listen for something that you can build on. Offer related facts from your own experience, something you've read, or heard. Ask an intelligent question or draw someone else into the mix. Be actively involved but do not dominate the conversation. Comprehend, reply or redirect.

If you meet an insult comedian or cynic who insists on negatively, dominating, Bullying, and spoiling the dinner conversation, give him or her subtle, positive counter punches all the while thinking, "I'm rubber, you're glue, whatever you say bounces off me and sticks to you." If his or her comments are directed to you. Respond with a brave answer. It doesn't really matter what you say as long as you respond with a question. Say something like, "Is that all?" to put the ball back in his or her court. When everyone at the table then looks at the bully, he or she will probably back off because bullies are anti-social and cowardly.

"I'm rubber, you're glue, insults bounce off me and stick to you."

Above all, remember that vulgar language in the dining room is strictly taboo! This includes: cursing and swearing of course, prejudiced, sexual and racist comments and jokes, potty mouth, medical complaints, descriptions of operations, illnesses and surgeries, accidents, wounds, injuries to humans and animals.

Avoid discussing death, divorce, religion and politics directly with new dinner party acquaintances. These subjects can trigger dramatic reaction which are not appropriate for table talk. However, if you want to get to know someone's views, skirt the issue by avoiding labels and get a fair idea of where they stand until you feel comfortable going further with the subject, perhaps it can be pursued, one-on-one, at another time. Remember, there may be others in your company who feel strongly about these issues. This why politics, for example, one of the biggest dinner conversation no-nos. Freedom of Speech in regards to politics comes down to casting your vote once, at elections on a sacred, secret ballot. Study ideologies, listen to all points of view and choose what you believe. If someone asks you about a nominee, a law or an issue, answer tactfully, in an informed, polite and non-confrontational way. When the time comes to campaign with like-minded individuals, we hear the call: "Now is the time for all good men (and women) to come to the aid of his (or her) party."

Conversations about religion can be tricky as well, because although we have rights to privacy and Freedom of Religion, some people express their beliefs and try to convert others at inappropriate times. Prepare yourself for intelligent conversations just in case the subject comes up. Educate yourself about the major religions and ethnic core beliefs or, avoid discussion by using tact. Redirect the conversation to legends of character, mythology or the concept of spiritual journey for a non-confrontational exchange on a similar theme.

For example, the following fable addresses character: A child asks, "When I grow up, will I be good or bad?" The parent replies, " You have two wolves within. One is good, the other is bad. The one you feed will survive."

Negative images can put others off their food and you. Ultimately, that would be an insult to your host and hostess. Rely on your collection of non-controversial subjects you know well to get to know others. If you run out of things to say, ask questions or simply tell your host, "Well, I don't want to bore you all. I have run out of conversation and it's getting late, it's time for me to go, the food was delicious! Thank you and Good night." At all costs, avoid getting into the last resort of poor conversationalists, the 'Top this One" gross-out stories.

Good etiquette and protocol training require that we introduce ourselves and others. (For more on Introductions, see Lesson Three-Protocol.) To introduce yourself, say, "I'm____." Have an opening line to start conversations with like, "I'm in customer service." Introductions will increase your circle of influence exponentially. Introductions strengthen your support system and help you to get ahead.

Use titles and names when you ask people a question. As in, "Mr. Martin, Please pass the salt and pepper." Also use titles when introducing two people and say the name of the older person, the person with higher rank or the closer friend first. When introducing a man and a woman, say the woman's name first, as in: "Ms. Dillon, I would like you to meet Mr. Martin ." or, "Good evening, Mrs. Branchard, thank you for inviting us, I'd like to introduce my cousin, Franklin."

One of the first steps in making a good impression is to remember the name of someone you just met. Say it again right away. Like, "Sit with us, Matt, we can talk more."Then say their name during the conversation. As in, "I think I understand what you mean, Matt." Then say the name again when you part. Like, "It was nice meeting you, Matt." This practice will imbed the name into your long-term memory. Write it down too as another aid to help later with recall. Collect and exchange business cards for back up. For a good impression, keep business cards in your jacket pocket, near your heart.

If you cannot recall someone's name and you want to introduce another to them, ask someone else whom you think will know that name before you start the introductions. Otherwise, start with the person whose name you know, tell them you'd like them to meet… gesture toward the unknown person, hesitate and give eye contact to the unknown person who at that point, will usually offer their name. If they don't jump in and say their name…go on with "…Sorry, I don't recall your name," or "…Your name is?" Even a rather awkward introduction is better than none at all. Introductions can be life-changing, they are important, a sign of good etiquette training and not doing them is simply to miss opportunities.

"Proper Introductions are a sign of good etiquette training."

It is good practice at formal affairs to use titles and surnames until you get acquainted. (Use nicknames with close friends and family only.) Practice using proper names when addressing friends and family at the dining table. This gets their attention and makes it clear to whom you are speaking. When passing things to each other and doing other little favors, say, "Please," "Thank you" and "You're welcome." Even at home these magic words are heartwarming ambassadors of etiquette training and sensitivity. Whether the host at the table or just a polite and considerate person, every member of a dinner party should make an effort to draw others into the table conversation with questions or anecdotes involving them and related to what is being said. For example, "Oh, that was a great game! It was so close! You were there, Andy, What was that score?" Sharing the talking time allows everyone time to eat. If one person tells a long, interesting story without another person politely interrupting, or without passing the conversation to another, so that he can take a few bites, his dinner might get cold or be taken away to make way for the next course. Remember, you are not invited to the table merely to be fed. You are there to dine and participate with others in the Art of Conversation. If you 'drop the ball' there will be an uncomfortable lapse in the conversation.

"Be Tactful."

In one-on-one encounters, to exercise even more skill in the Art of Conversation, show deeper confidence and good character by adding these phrases to your repertoire: " I'm sorry" and "I forgive you." Along with this train of thought, one of the hardest tasks for any of us is to give or take criticism, yet it is sometimes necessary. Be tactful When you feel obligated to correct someone's behavior, always preface your comments with a phrase something like, "I don't mean to be rude, or embarrass you." This will give the person you are addressing forewarning and allow them to brace for impact of what you have to say. Knowing it is not a hostile confrontation, they are likely to listen politely. This technique is a reliable buffer for your own emotions too, like counting to ten when one's temper is tested.

International Travel

Nothing is more highly appreciated in a foreign country than the visitor's efforts to learn and speak even a few words in the local language. In fact, it is considered standard protocol to greet foreigners in their own tongue whether we are visiting abroad or when they come here. Unless both sides make an effort, immigrants may seem reluctant to assimilate and therefore stay unto themselves in an attempt at recreating their homeland. In time we will see that Earth's culture can sustain and embrace all peoples. Earth's culture, this global melting pot invites us all to speak at least a few words and phrases in many languages! Here are some important international greetings and phrases to start with:

Greetings

English	Hello	Goodbye	Thank you
French:	bonjour	au revoir	merci
Spanish:	hola	adios	gracias
German:	guten tag	auf wiedersehen	danke
Italian:	buon giorno	ciao	grazie
Russian:	privet	dosvidanjia	spasibo
Portuguese:	ola	adeus	obrigado
Chinese:	nei hao	zai jian	xie xie nei
Japanese:	ohio gozimas	sayonara	arigato

Lesson Six - Conversation - Activity

Learn to say Hello, Good Bye and Thank you in five languages.

T. K. Reilly

Lesson Six - Conversation - Crossword Puzzle

Down:
2. mild flattery. 3. drop the ball. 5. big grin. 7. anecdote. 8. hostess gift.

Across:
1. non-confrontational. 4. good listener. 6. coward. 9. magic word.
10 vulgar language. 11 melting pot.

Conversation

Complete the puzzle.

Lesson Seven

CORRESPONDENCE

When my sixth grade Math teacher gave a pop quiz, he would say, "Get out your napkins, we are going to have a picnic!" This is not a pop quiz, however, you will need pen and paper because this lesson is about creative writing.

Consider for a moment those glowing screens we have learned to love so much. They give us information, entertainment, news, comfort and access to others. I believe connectedness is a good thing, an obsession like fire that is helping mankind to evolve. However, "Mobile connectedness has eroded fundamental human courtesies," as Anthony De Rosa, Social Media writer at Reuters, has said; and, in a New York Times article, David Carr elaborates on the subject[1]. Clearly, people know that they must delay their devices at times. But we have to do better than that. Heed Mr. De Rosa's warning and employ etiquette and protocol in your online presence and everyday activities. Learn to behave, stop the erosion and strengthen fundamental human courtesies in our culture.

Texts, Tweets, Skype, phone conversations and emails on companion media do not deliver the lasting social impression of written correspondence like letters, and personal notes. Hand written correspondence is filtered through the mental and physical processes of artful composition, editing, proofreading and penmanship. Hand written correspondence is often meant for permanent records, scrapbooks, even frames. Above all, in the modern world of mobile devices and expediency, the last vestige of hand written, short and sweet correspondence is…

---

1 David Carr, "Keep Your Thumbs Still When I'm Talking to You, " the New York Times, April 15, 2011. http://www.nytimes.com/2011/04/17/fashion/17TEXT.html

The Thank You Note

Keep a fountain pen, fine stationery or monogrammed note cards, postage stamps and a book of phrases on hand and at the ready. Practice good penmanship for artful compositions. Thoughtful Thank You notes are a sign of good etiquette and protocol training. Every thank you note is appreciated whether emailed preprinted or hand-made. But of course, handwritten is best.

Quite honestly, Thank You notes fulfill an important purpose. They give closure. They are the desired response. Without them, an important transaction is left open-ended creating a vacuum into which the best intentions can fall silent and unrequited. Best to follow any gift, interview, reception and important act of kindness with a Thank You note written and dispatched within three days, short, sweet and to the point.

An efficient Thank You note contains up to six points of interest:

1.) Open with a friendly or creative greeting like, Dear Harold, Dearest friend, Honored Client, Highly Esteemed Associate, Best New Customer, etc, followed by the receiver's name. 2.) Describe the gift or reason for the note. For example: "Thank you for the fine fountain pen." 3.) Add any appropriate additional information that will help express your appreciation: "I will use it exclusively when important documents require my signature!" 4.) Close with a phrase or additional comment, like: "Thank you for taking time out of your busy schedule to meet with us and celebrate the mutual success of our companies." 5.) End thank You notes with friendly closing such as: Sincerely, Your friend, Warm regards, Yours truly, etc. 6.) Lastly, Sign your first name in cursive and in ink.

> *"Thank You notes are a sign of good etiquette."*

Take care that your Thank You note conveys the message of gratitude intended. It should invoke in the receiver the same level of appreciation you felt when you received their gift. In business, many gifts are simply obligatory, and so is the acknowledgement or reciprocation of the gift. Some people say, "It is better to give than to receive." and "It's the thought that counts." Implying that Thank You Notes are not necessary, but they really are. Every gift is given with the notion that the receiver will like or appreciate it and the effort that went into selecting and sending it. Without a proper thank you, there may be a lingering doubt that the gift was liked. The giver may doubt their judgment in giving a gift to you, and may not be inclined repeat the favor. The giver may have to wonder even if the gift has been received. A verbal thank you or e-card, is not quite the same, too easy. Remember that many actions done in the name of etiquette and protocol are purely reciprocal. In building relationships, good will and networking the following is true:

"Actions speak louder than words."

Creating anxiety or doubt in someone who was nice enough or smart enough to give a gift, is not polite, especially in the everyday give and take of the business world where someone is always keeping score. Do not procrastinate and forget to write Thank You Notes, personal, hand-written notes are ties that bind.

Giving thanks and giving toasts

When there is a moment of quiet to give thanks…BE QUIET! When there is a toast everyone usually stands. We always raise our glass or water goblet and sip with a toast, it's considered rude not to. If the toast is for you, stand, smile and say "Thank you." Do not raise a glass to toast yourself. Do not applaud yourself. If you are the guest of honor, be prepared to say, "Thank you all for coming, I really appreciate you all." Or something to that effect, as the saying goes:

"With speeches: Be brief and be seated."

Invitations

When you host an event, you need to provide your guests with the four W's. Who is the host/hostess and who is the guest of honor? What is the occasion? When is the event? Where is the event? Also tell guests who to respond or 'RSVP' to if they are planning to attend and tell them what Attire will be appropriate for the event. If you receive an invitation and cannot attend, call anyway to convey your regrets. Guests should reply three - five days before an event so the host knows how many guests to plan for. Invitations should go out at least two weeks before an event. (For weddings and reunions, allow up to three months for guests who have to make travel plans.)

Lesson Activity - Hand-Written Notes

Jack and Jill, find a page in the back of the book. I would like you to use it to write proper Thank You Notes to each other for fabulous, imaginary birthday gifts. Leave room to write a second note too.

Would you like to hear what we wrote when we finish?

Yes, please, of course. I know you are a good writer, Jack.
Oh, you mean my email, right?
Yes. Thank you. Here is my Thank You Note:

To My Dear Sister, Jill,
Once again, I am so grateful to you for my amazing birthday gift. Thank you for the talking parrot! It is a constant source of amusement and a terrific pet! I will let you know when I come up with the perfect name for it. You never fail with your originality and creative choice of gifts. Thank you very much!
Your OLDER brother,
Jack

That's very good. I especially liked the clever reference to your age in the closing. I like a well placed pun. As Shakespeare said, "Brevity is the soul of wit."

Now, I would like you to use the rest of the page to write a proper Sympathy Note to someone who is in mourning. Use the same format of six points as for a Thank You, but with different contents of course: Use pen and ink, A polite greeting, Name the deceased, Tell something you liked about them and say, "I am sorry for your loss." End with a polite closing.

Jill, While Jack is writing, let's hear your Thank You Note.

Dearest Jack,
Thank you for the delightful butterfly garden. I was skeptical when you put it under my window. But now, only a few days later, watching it is my favorite past time. Lots of butterflies visit each day. You should see it!
Your loving Sister,
Jill

Nice job, Jill. I think your note conveys the range of emotion such a gift would naturally evoke. It also contains a good visual message. Please go ahead and compose a sympathy note too.

Your turn to read again, Jack.

Dear Wendell,
We were all so sorry to hear about your Dad's passing. Mr. Whitman was the best Scout Master ever. I mean, when he spoke to the troop it was like he was addressing the men we would be some day. He believed in us. He will be missed. I am truly sorry for your loss.
Your friend,
Jack

Well done, Jack. I think your note delivers the intended condolence. It is personal and comforting. Jill, let's hear yours?

Dear Toby,
I can't believe that Bingo escaped! I can't believe he ran away. Don't worry, he is a smart dog and I am sure he has found another loving home. Please accept my sympathy, I am sorry for your loss.
Your friend,
Jill

Good point, the loss of a pet is life changing for people and they deserve sympathy. Thank you. By the way, we should all really find the time to practice our penmanship. Old fashioned, spidery script is out of fashion now. The modern trends in cursive I have observed show less connectivity, more rounded consonants, shorter ascenders and descenders in the lower case and less lofty capitals. It is important to show a consistent slant to your handwriting for the convenience of the reader's eye. Take pride in your hand writing, it is as unique as your signature.

"Personal, Hand-written Notes are Ties that Bind"

Lesson Seven, Correspondence - Quiz

1. What is the purpose of a Thank You Note? _____.

2. What are the six points of a proper Thank You Note? _____
_____
_____
_____.

3. When is a Thank You Note appropriate? _____
_____
_____.

4. How long should you wait before you send a Thank You Note? _____
_____.

5. What are the six points of a proper Sympathy Note? _____
_____
_____
_____
_____.

6. _____ speak louder than words.

7. What are the four W's of a proper invitation? _____
_____
_____
_____.

8. What additional information is required on an invitation? _____
_____.

9. Invitations should go out at least _____ weeks before an event.

10. How many days before the event does the host need to know the number of guests to expect? _____.

Lesson Eight

DINING ETIQUETTE

Hello, You both look great in your 'black tie' attire.

Thank you, you do too. We skipped ahead to Lesson Eleven on Formal Attire when we received your invitation. Wow, there is a dining table here.

I also invited some other guests for dinner. Thank you for the bouquet, it will make a nice centerpiece.

Welcome everyone. Etiquette allows wildly diverse souls with identical sets of utensils and social skills, to engaged in polite conversation while dining. Before the meal however, protocol requires that introductions be made so that members of the party can converse on a first name basis.

Seating

At formal tables, you may have a name card at your seat. The seating arrangement will be lady, gentleman, lady, etc. To move the cards would be improper. When Dinner time is announced, gentlemen offer to escort ladies into the room, extending the right elbow for her to take his arm or his right forearm, (in which case she would lay her forearm and hand atop his). He says, "May I escort you to your seat?" Gentlemen help the ladies with their chairs by pulling the chair out from the table, the lady then steps in front of the chair and the gentleman pushes the chair in until it touches the back of her knees, she controls her own distance from the table by taking hold of the sides of the seat of the chair to pull it under her as she sits. She then thanks the gentleman and he takes his seat. In formal situations, gentlemen stand and/or assist with chairs when a lady enters the room or when she leaves the table. Attire will tell you the level of formality of each affair. *(see lesson eleven)*

Watch your host and follow his example. If you are at a no host table, pace yourself with others and listen to the Master of Ceremonies (MC) so that you will not miss a cue.

Most of us eat fast food in the car one day, order- in and sit on the couch in front of the TV next day, blend, drink or microwave our nutrition on the run while scouting out dishes to cook or grill at home when we have the time. Obviously formal dining is different. Because when seated at a dining table you and every other member of the party have a place setting and table partners in front of you; the scene is *set* for the social experience of dining. Place settings define our personal working space with tools for the job of dining. The basic place setting has 6 parts. Placement of these parts is traditional and predictable. Each piece of the place setting has rules that come with it to insure that you dine using good table manners. Dining etiquette allows us to feed ourselves without offending anyone, while engaged in the exchange of useful or entertaining information.

A common offense might be to take a drink from someone else's beverage or help yourself to the bread on their bread plate because you don't know or can't remember which side of the place setting your bread plate is on. Memorize the following rhyme to remember the precise location of each item in your place setting:

Place Setting Rhyme

**Hey Diddle Diddle…
My plate in the Middle
And we'll be eating soon.
My fork on the Left…
Below the bread plate…
Across from my cup and spoon.
My knife on the Right,
Its blade facing in…
And now we can begin.**

Napkins

Please wait until everyone is seated before you begin to eat. Generally, when you sit down at the table, the first thing to do is put your napkin on your lap. If there is a host or hostess at your table, wait until he or she deploys the napkin and takes the first bite of food, then follow their example. If you must leave the table temporarily during a meal, place your napkin on your chair. It would be highly irregular to have the following occur in fine dining, but if in the course of the meal, something like gristle, seeds or a an olive pit must be removed from your mouth, make it as small as possible first and then bring the corner of your napkin up to your mouth and push the item out onto the napkin with your tongue as you appear to wipe your mouth or make a small cough. It is not considered polite to put the fingers into the mouth while dining, especially to extract something and it is equally bad form to stack up refuse on the bread plate as some do. Roll up the napkin, concealing the item or excuse yourself to the washroom where you can privately expectorate and rinse your mouth. When you are done eating, place your napkin to the left of your plate.

Your napkin's main job is to protect your clothing and keep your fingers and mouth clean. Remember it is not a bib, tissue, mop, sponge, hat, shawl, handkerchief or a flag. Occasionally dab the corners of your mouth and your chin where bits of food can hide with the corner of your napkin. Check your chest for crumbs and drips now and then to keep yourself tidy.

To keep your smile presentable, discreetly rinse the teeth with a sip of water and swallow. (It is not polite to swish, gargle, smack the lips, pick, or clean your teeth in public.) If someone else has a problem, like spinach stuck on the front teeth or sauce on their chin, for example, and you want to help them, tell them quietly and discreetly by establishing eye contact and then point to your own tooth or chin. Hopefully they will catch on quickly, appreciate your thoughtfulness and return the favor if needed. If your glass is spilled, ask for a waiter's help cleaning-up and do your best not to make a fuss about it. If someone else spills do the same and avoid embarrassing them by using your napkin to blot his or her chest and lap.

Bread and Butter

Waiters will bring water and bread and butter first or these may already be on the table when you arrive. Nibble while waiting for others to arrive, but don't overdo it. To eat bread and butter politely: First acquire a personal supply of butter and place it on your bread plate. All types of bread, rolls and butter reside on the bread plate and are eaten in bite-sized pieces taken one at a time. If you take bread from a basket on the table, pass it next to the person on your right. Hold the bread in one hand and break off a piece with the other. Apply a small amount of butter with your spreader or dip specialty breads like Faccocia into the pool of seasoned oil provided and pop that bite of bread into your mouth. A dinner roll should provide three to ten bites eaten this way. With not much in your mouth you can swallow quickly, answer someone who may speak to you and enjoy conversation while leaving room in your stomach for dinner. Again, eat small bites, one at a time and swallow before you open your mouth. We all know the admonition:

"Don't Talk with Food in Your Mouth."

Foods are served in a certain order of "courses." Detailed information about courses is described later in this lesson. Specific utensils (also known as flatware) and stemware are laid in the place setting specifically for use in eating foods in coming courses. Formal place settings have more than one fork, knife and spoon. Each utensil is a tool used for eating certain types of food. We start with the outermost utensils and work our way toward the ones nearest the dinner plate. Forks on the left, knives and spoons on the right. Note: the fish fork is placed on the right with other knives because though it has a prong or *tine* for removal of fish bones, its primary feature is a blade for cutting fish. The knife, fork and spoon are tools we use for dining. Like any other tools, patience and practice are required to become skilled at using them.

Stemware

In your place setting, all the stem wear for your drinks is positioned at the upper right of your plate above your knives and spoons. There, you might find a champagne flute, a smaller, stemmed glass for white wine, a larger, red wine stem and a bigger, rounder, stemmed water goblet. Wine glasses are used, when appropriate wines are paired with courses: typically Champagne for toasts, White wines for the Fish Course and Red or Rose wines are served with the meat course.

Food Service

In formal dining rooms, food is served in one of the following ways:

Plate Service: (*often called American Ser*vice) Whether or not the food intended for the meal has been displayed first, each individual plate of food is made up in the kitchen and then brought to the table.

Sideboard Service: (a *high narrow table standing by the dining room wall, near the dining table*) Each plate is filled by the waiter, or Butler/Maid, at the Sideboard and then brought to the guest.

English Service: Food platters are presented on a table or cart. Seated guests serve themselves from serving platters held by waiters. When guests are asked to serve themselves from side tables, it is referred to as a Buffet.

Family Style Service: Various foods intended for the meal are placed on the table in serving dishes. Each individual will serve himself and then pass it on. In this case, we pass the serving platters to our right. Remember, service always comes in from the left and moves on and out to the right.

French or Russian Service: This style of service is considered the epitome of elegance and is the one traditionally used formally in the White House. White-gloved staff serves each guest from silver platters.

DINNER COURSES

Seven - Course Banquet
preceded by a social hour/cocktail hour with appetizers
... 1st a Soup course
2nd a **Fish Course** (served with white wine)
3rd a **Sorbet Course**
4th a **Meat Course** (red or white meat, paired with red or rose wine)
5th a **Salad Course**
6th **the Dessert Course** (champagne for toasting)
7th **Course, the Coffee Course** (after-dinner-drinks)
(note: a Five - Course Banquet omits fish and sorbet courses)

The cocktail hour not only gives everyone time relax and greet others, it also allows guests time to check their coats and wraps, get their parking receipt validated, check-in with the reception table, perhaps get name tags and banquet table numbers. You may even pose for photos and still have time to visit the restroom to wash hands before dinner is announced and the gentlemen escort the ladies through the doors into the dining room.

The Basic Banquet Program

Most banquets use the following agenda. Once guests are settled in their chairs, Host and Hostess or Master of Ceremonies will call for everyone's attention. Everyone waits for the Host to welcome the guests to the banquet. There may be a pause to say a blessing or give thanks for the meal. After the blessing and the welcoming, everyone puts their napkins on their lap and the meal begins.

Remember your manners when making requests, passing bread, breaking and eating bread politely, sipping your soup quietly, slicing meats toward you with a stroking, not sawing, motion and if noodles are served, wind them onto the tip of your fork. Sit up straight and keep your elbows at your sides.

If the meal is especially messy, like lobster for which you may need a bib, for example. After the meat course, you may receive a finger bowl (a bowl of water used for rinsing the fingers) before dessert. It will be placed in front of you on your dessert plate. As a visual clue to its identity, sometimes a rose petal will be floating in it. A dessert fork and spoon may be with it.

To use a finger bowl…Dip the fingertips of each hand in turn into the bowl and dry them with your napkin. When finished, lift the bowl with both hands and place it on the table to your upper left. If you do not need the finger bowl at the moment, move it and wait for salad and dessert to be served. Then wash your fingertips after dessert so that your hands will certainly be clean before dancing begins.

Champagne may be served at the beginning of the banquet and a toast may be made then and again as the 6th course, the Dessert Course is served. This time, the toast will be to the Guest of Honor, or for a special announcement. Lastly, with the 7th course, cups and saucers for coffee and tea and a bowl of nuts or chocolate candies containing nuts to provide a balance of protein to the caffeine jitters from the chocolate, coffee and tea. Thus the Seven-Course meal provides everything from *Soup to Nuts!*

After dessert, ladies may excuse themselves to reapply lipstick, perfume and comb or brush hair. It is considered impolite to apply make-up at the dining table. Everyone should go to the restroom at some point after the salad course to rinse their mouth, check their teeth and hair, wash hands, etc., you will want to look your best at a banquet after the sixth course when music and dancing begin.

Traditional banquet dance programs will start with classic ballroom dances and phase into contemporary music.

Lesson Eight - Dining Etiquette - Activity

1. Memorize and recite the Place Setting Rhyme
2. Name the courses in a seven-course banquet, including wines.

Lesson Nine

THE CONCERT STYLE OF DINING

Jill, I think this lesson will address your comments about issues with how Jack was holding a fork while dining.

Thank you! I've been looking forward to hearing this lesson.

Knife and Fork

With practice, even youngsters can slice foods and dine using the knife and fork together quietly and efficiently with ease. Hold the fork in your left hand, the knife in your right, extending your pointer fingers along the back of each utensil. The fork should be held tines down with the tip of your finger at the top, back side of the fork where the tines are joined to the body of the fork. Hold the knife blade down of course with your finger firmly along its spine and the tip of your finger at its collar. The bottom of each utensil should be held against the palm, by the other fingers.

There are three styles of slicing and eating with knife and fork. They are: Continental, American and Concert. In each style, the utensils are held as described above, with the possible exception of an alternate, American style slicing position in which the fork is held vertically, facing the diner, with supporting fingers in the back and the thumb in the front. The following is a description of dining techniques and custom associated with each style.

In Continental (or European) style, both hands are kept visible with wrists resting on the edge of the table. The fork is held, tines down, in the left hand throughout the meal. As such, It holds food in place for slicing and to carry it to the mouth. Foods such as vegetables are pressed by the tip of the knife onto back of the fork for delivery.

For American style, start in this way, then the knife is placed blade-in, on the dinner plate at the top after cutting each bite. (Historically, this custom was a point of honor and graciousness, not having to hold one's knife throughout the meal, also to not be required to keep both hands in full view on the table). After cutting a bite and laying down the knife, the fork is transferred from left to right hand for picking up the bite just cut and feeding oneself while the left hand rests in the lap. This is a slower style of eating because of time spent shifting utensils so may be conductive to good digestion but repeatedly placing the knife down on the edge of the dinner plate may be noisy.

In Concert style dining, we start with Continental style for slicing three or four bites eaten one at a time from down-turned tines at the end of the fork just after cutting. This is done with the knife still held in the right hand, wrist resting on the table edge. After slicing and eating a few bites, put the knife down at the top of the plate, blade in-facing, until it is needed again. Continue dining using American style. Transfer the fork, tines up, to the right hand and serve yourself or *graze* on potatoes and vegetables with the fork in the right hand, your left hand in your lap or holding a *pusher or* piece of bread. To be ready for the next slicing job, the fork may be placed temporarily on the left surface of the plate, tines up while you pause, to take a sip of water a bite of bread, or perhaps begin or enter a conversation.

Whichever style of dining you choose, remember to keep used utensils on the plate.

"Once utensils have been used, they must not be replaced on the table nor left jutting out from the side of the plate like oars on a rowboat." (Tiffany's Table Manners for Teen-Agers")

When taking a longer break during the meal, place the knife and fork, tines down, in the X position across your plate. This signals the waiter that you have not yet finished eating. When you have finished, place the knife and fork together diagonally across the plate in a position resembling ten-minutes-to-four on the face of a clock. This is the signal that you have finished dining and request plate removal. Remember it as: 10 - 4, or the diagonal line across a circle, (\) the universal signal for NO, take it away, I am finished with it. over and out. To help prevent the utensils from sliding off the plate when it is lifted from the table, the knife blade should be placed between the tines of the fork and the fork set on its side.

All meats such as steak, turkey, chicken and fish and many fruits and vegetables should be cut and eaten one bite at a time. When the main course is presented, begin with the meat. With a downward insertion of the fork, hold the meat in place and then with the knife behind the fork, slice the meat, pressing down and cutting toward you - with stroking motions to avoid the appearance of sawing wood.

Concert Style

"Hold fast, while I slice and stack food on your head. Said the Knife to the Fork, Please stay."

The Fork replied, " Continental? No way, not today. I hope to convert your mind. After each cut, in the States we say, the Fork changes hands, it is our way. Knives must wait at the top of the plate while Forks clean the plate and graze. Don't pile food on the top of my head, I can get it myself with my tines."

"I see what you mean, he opined, to lay down the Knife is a peacemaking sign. Yet there is a way that could be nice, combine techniques, I ask you thrice, Work with me for the first four bites, we'll do it your way the next nine."

If we compromise by working in concert, the best of both worlds will evolve. The room will be quiet, there won't be a riot and this awkwardness will dissolve. Out with the old ways and in with the new. You and I are the style makers now."

"I agree, said the fork, I'll stay with you 'til the slicing part of the meal is through. At a leisurely rate, while you take a break, I'll work alone for a while."

Old habits reborn in the hands of the young feel like nature and go with the flow, Now everyone's doing this new way of dining. I call it the Concert Style.

Lesson Nine - The Concert Style - Activity - Slicing Practice

Practice slicing and eating in the Concert Style.

Lesson Nine - The Concert Style - Quiz

On the page below, draw the signals given with the knife and fork to waiters to indicate when you are **A.** resting during a meal and want to keep your plate and **B.** when you are finished and would like them to take away your plate.

A. at rest = _____ , **B.** finished = _____

Lesson Ten

CONNOISSEUR

Hello, you know this is all starting to sink in. Allot of these lessons actually seem familiar somehow.

That's good news, Jack. I'm glad to hear it, and it is beginning to show too.

After all, as a member of a living culture you are immersed in its way of life.

You already know much more than you think you do. Let's bring more to light…

A true connoisseur knows the foods of different countries, even the foods and beverages of different regions in different countries. The following samples of menus from French, Italian and Chinese restaurants for example, offer a range of dishes with distinctive tastes, ingredients and styles of preparation. This lesson features Italian French and Chinese menus because these the most popular types of restaurants serving foods outside our comfort zone. A confident host and hostess can decipher menus different from the usual fare.

To become more sophisticated, educate your palate. Develop a sense of taste by gradually sampling items on the menu until you can order and cook in a particular genre to your own liking. Every adult should have a working knowledge of popular international foods, especially if you entertain socially or for business. Ladies generally order first. So, Jill, this is a 'heads up'. Ladies especially should know what they like so that they can order quickly and not delay the meal.

Italian Food

An Italian *Trattoria* is a medium-priced, often family-run eating establishment where large tables are shared, family-style. A typical Italian dinner is presented in the following order: "L'antipasto" means *before the meal*. This hot and cold appetizer includes greens, cheese and meats on a plate. " Il Primo", or First course, usually consists of pasta and "Zuppa," meaning, soup, like Minestrone, "Risotto," rice cooked in a broth." Al dente," means, *to the tooth*, or slightly crisp and chewy as a preferred way of cooking pasta. Il Secondo", or "Second course," is the main course of meat, poultry, game or fish, like "Cuscus alla Trapanese, a seafood couscous dish from Trapani, Chicken Cacciatore, chicken pieces simmered in a tomato sauce with mushrooms and served over pasta, or "Rosticciana," Tuscan- style, barbecued pork ribs". "Il Contorno," or side dishes consist of vegetables such as "Melanzane," (Eggplant) like "Caponata" a sweet and sour eggplant ragout dish from Sicily, "Spinaci," Spinach, or "Insalata mista," mixed salad. "Ildolce", or dessert, includes such favorite sweets as "Gelato" creamy, flavored ices, "Tiramisu,"a layered confection of coffee soaked ladyfingers , Mascarpone cheese, Marsala wine, sugar, eggs and whipped cream, "Zabaglione," a custard of egg yolks with wine and brandy or "Canollis," Sicilian pastry tubes filled with cream, great with Cappuccino, and Espresso. Water and Italian bread or bread sticks are served with the meal.

French Cuisine

French restaurants may feature a "Plat du jour," or daily special, this typically includes meat, vegetables and perhaps potatoes, all for one price. In a French restaurant, chicken is "Poulet," beef is "Boeuf" and fish is " Poisson." To order, start with an "Entree." After the "Entree," you may choose one of the "Plats Principaux," or main dishes of your preference. Many of these terms will be familiar. For example, "Filet Mignon" is a small, tender steak, "Bouillabaisse" is fish stew (from Provence),"Le Boeuf Bourguignon" is beef stew (from Burgundy), "Poulet a l'ail" is chicken with garlic. Of course, "Les Escargot" are land snails cooked in butter and garlic and "Les Cuisses de Grenouille" are frog legs, breaded and fried. Order vegetables from the "Legumes." Some side dishes are, "Ariz" and "Pommes" or rice and potatoes. "Fromage," or cheese, is served after the main course.

"Souffles" and "Quiches" are egg- pies. "La soupe a l'oignon" is French onion soup. "Fondu" is a heated, cheese or chocolate sauce, you dip bite-sized pieces of meat or fruit on long forks, into. French pastries and desserts include: "Creme Brulee" custard with carmelized sugar glaze; Napóleons and Petite Fours (tiny cakes), chilled delicacies like chocolate Mousse and Parfaits; or

"Crepes," thin, pancakes with various fruit fillings and toppings. (Note, crepes are also served as a main dish filled with meat or seafood). You may also enjoy Crepes Suzette or Cherries Jubilee, famously flamed with Cognac or Brandy. Bread (sliced French baguette) comes with each meal. To ask for water, say: "Un carafe d'eau." Bon Appetit!

Chinese Food

As with all restaurants, you know a Chinese restaurant is especially good if there is a line at the door every day. A typical Chinese meal begins with appetizers such as Egg rolls, Spring rolls or Deep fried wontons. Continue with soup such as: Egg Drop Soup, Hot and Sour Soup or Wonton Soup (meat and vegetables floating in little "clouds." A family dinner is usually made up of four or five main dishes plus big bowls of white rice. The Father or host is served first, then he serves or everyone partakes from serving dishes as they go by on a revolving "lazy Susan" tray in the center of the table.

Chinese dishes are made with sliced meats mixed with steamed vegetables and tasty sauces such as: Beef in Oyster Sauce, Beef with Broccoli, Sweet and Sour Chicken, Lemon Chicken "Ling Mung Gai," Crispy Skin Duck "Xang Su Ya" and Fish in Hot Sauce "Dou Ban Yu." General Tsao's Chicken is cubed, coated in cornstarch, deep-fried and served in a dark sauce with chili peppers. If you like hot, spicy foods, order from the Szechuan items on the menu, seasoned with chili peppers and peppercorns from Szechuan province of South Central China. Be sure to ask before ordering. "Mein" means noodles as in: "Chow Mein" or fried noodles with vegetables and meat and "Lo Mein" tossed noodles with sauce. Fried Rice is previously cooked rice combined with scrambled egg, vegetables and meat. "Moo Goo Gai Pan" is Stir-fried chicken and mushrooms and "Mu Shu Pork" is stir-fried, marinated pork mixed with bits of scrambled egg and sprouts served with plum sauce and pancakes for wrapping, eggroll - style. Meals are served with traditional chop sticks and Green Tea. Fortune cookies are a treat invented and added in America.

Steak House

If you like meat and potatoes, and you are ordering dinner in a steak house, you will be asked what size and which "Cut." Choose according to your appetite, the type of steak you like and how you like your steak prepared. For example, 8 oz., 9oz. or 16 oz. The most typical cuts, in descending order of price are: the Filet Mignon (usually 9 oz.), The New York Strip and the Rib Eye. There are three main choices of how you might like it prepared: Rare, Medium and Well-Done. They seem self-explanatory but if you order the popular "Medium" be sure that only the center is still pink. A well-done steak will be cooked through and tan inside and a rare steak is very juicy and reddish at its center. A less expensive but still very tasty steak, Prime Rib comes in 8 oz. ½ lb. and one or two pound cuts. You may also choose a "Kabob," chunks of steak on skewers with chunks of vegetables and fruit. Caesar Salad or Iceberg lettuce with Bleu cheese dressing is usually served before the main course. Your steak with come with your choice of baked and garnished, mashed or thick, fried potatoes. Desserts are often chosen from an elaborate display on a tray. Favorites include: New York style Cheese cake, Chocolate cake, Apple, Boston Cream, Coconut Cream, Cherry or Key Lime Pie, Chocolate fudge Brownies, or Strawberry short cake. Bread and water come with the meal.

For a better understanding of this lesson, obtain menus from fine dining establishments. These are easily acquired on-line. Practice alternately playing the Server and the Ordering Guest in turn to further demonstrate your understanding of the foods and the menus. To truly educate your fine dining palate, continue to expand your research to include other delicious foods and dining customs we do not have room for in this lesson including: Greek, Spanish, Lebanese, Japanese, Indian, Thai, German, Irish, Russian, Polish, etc. Each country offers meals with meat, vegetables and starches prepared and presented in various ways.

Cocktail Hour

Before a banquet there is always a social hour also known as the cocktail hour, cocktail party, cocktail reception or happy hour, held generally between 5 - 6 o'clock pm. This pre-function time allows guests to gather before dinner and visit, network or introduce new friends and it provides late-comers a better chance to arrive on time to the actual dinner event. During the cocktail hour, guests will enjoy a variety of before dinner drinks or aperitifs and appetizers to stimulate the appetite.

However, this is a matter of personal choice. If you are under pressure to drink but feel more comfortable not drinking, by all means, do what is best for you and do not drink alcohol. Although the following section goes into great detail about the contents of adult beverages, I don't mean to imply that you must join the others and drink alcohol. My intention is to give you the benefit of scientific information so that you can be intelligent, as a true connoisseur, about drinking and know its effects on people. After all, "Nam et ipsa potestas est., Knowledge is Power," (Sir Francis Bacon, 1597.) You can

Behave!

always order ginger ale, iced tea or non-alcoholic versions of adult beverages and maintain sobriety. Again, this is a matter of personal choice.

Jack, your email reminds us that the key to enjoying adult beverages is to drink in moderation and pace yourself. The rule to remember is, "One drink per hour."

I'm sure I can do it now, I really think I am ready now to be the guy who drinks one drink per hour or none at all!

That means, one beer, one glass of wine or one shot of hard liquor, per hour. Do yourself a favor and learn the following scientific facts.

Depending upon the occasion for the banquet, before-dinner drinks range from Champagne and white wines to cocktails and shots. The alcohol content in **Champagne** averages around 13% with bubbles to accelerate the effects while a wine cooler (white wine diluted with soda and ice) has about 7% alcohol content. (At 3.8 - 8%, **Beer** has a lower to higher alcohol content per its color. Beer is not usually served in a fine dining venue because its strong taste tends to overpower the palate.) A four ounce glass of White wine like **Chardonnay** (dry), **Chablis or Sauterne** (sweet) averages about 10 - 12.5% alcohol content respectively, Red wines vary from **Rose** (8%), **Cabernet Sauvignon** and **Chianti** and **Merlot** (friuty) at 11-13%. **Zinfandels** (17 - 22%) and **Port** at (20%) are slightly higher in alcohol. Fortified wines can contain up to 17% alcohol. Of course, four ounce cocktails made with hard liquor and straight shots of 1.5 oz 80 proof **Tequila** or 1 oz 100 proof **Vodka** spirits contain the highest alcohol contents of 40% and 50% alcohol respectively. Different brands of spirits contain different levels of potency. **Sake**, a Japanese adult beverage, contains 15 % alcohol, is served heated for quick effect.

The term "Drink Responsibly" means know what you are drinking and what to expect from drinking it so that you can stay in control and behave well while drinking. This calls for a scientific approach. A Zero BAC or Blood Alcohol Content means that you are sober. A BAC of .08 grams per deciliter (g/dl), is considered the legal limit for drinking and driving. A twelve oz beer containing 5% alcohol per oz, a 5oz glass of wine containing 12% alcohol per oz and 1 1/2 oz shot of Tequilla containing 40% alcohol, all have about the same alcohol content. Learn to maximize the positive effects of alcohol by keeping your BAC down to .06. Again, you should be able to accomplish this by imbibing one drink per hour in a four hour period. That means, one beer, one glass of wine or one shot of hard liquor, per hour.

We know that the first alcoholic beverage produces a positive, euphoric, feeling or "buzz," but once the BAC reaches .06, you are at what is known as the ***point of diminishing returns*** after which one begins to feel the negative effects of alcohol including sluggishness, slurred speech and lack of balance making you appear drunk to others and inhibiting your ability to function properly. These facts are irrefutable and apply to everyone. Your BAC rises according to the number of ounces of alcohol consumed, your body size, how much you've had to eat, the percentage of fat on your body, temperature and quality of the alcholic beverage and your gender. Various formulas exist to calculate BAC. The easiest way to measure BAC is with a breathalyzer test. The best way to control it is with common sense, remember:

"One drink per hour takes will power."

Become intelligent about adult beverages. Knowing the ingredients is in your cocktail will help you make your best choice and ultimately do your best under the influence of its alcoholic content. Knowing what you like will help you pace yourself through an evening's imbibing. Do you like sweet, sour, tart or fruit flavored drinks? Do you like your drink with or without ice, chilled, room temperature or heated? How thirsty are you? Do you like gulping down lots of liquid or sipping only a little? Know your preferences and your drinking style. After one cocktail you could pace yourself with a non-alcoholic beverage for example, allowing you to stay within the one drink per hour limit and also enjoy a glass of wine and water with dinner and then perhaps an after dinner drink as well.

Adult drinking is a privilege, don't spoil it by overdoing it or doing it ignorantly. If you have had your limit and someone offers to 'top off' or 'freshen-up' your drink, put your hand over the glass and simply say, "No, thank you." No amount of peer pressure should convince you to embarrass yourself and jeopardize your job, your relationships and corrupt the status of your good character by becoming intoxicated and losing self control. The following will help further educate the privileged pallet with a scientific approach to keeping Cocktail Hour *Happy*.

Popular Cocktails

The **Martini** contains 3 oz Gin (94 proof - 47% alcohol) and 1/2 oz **Vermouth**. (If Vermouth is dry it contains 16% alcohol, sweet - 18% alcohol.) The Gin and Vermouth are shaken (or stirred if you prefer) in crushed ice, strained into a chilled martini glass and garnished with an olive for dry Martini or a cherry for a sweet one.

The **Gimlet** containing 3 1/2 oz Gin or Vodka (100 proof - 50% alcohol) and 1 oz of lime juice to taste, shaken in an ice-filled cocktail shaker and strained into a chilled cocktail glass. The invention of this drink is attributed to Dr. Gimlette of the British Royal Navy who created it in 1890 to make sailors more willing to drink lime juice that contained vitamin C for their health.

The **Cosmopolitan** contains 1 oz Vodka with equal parts: cranberry juice, lime juice and **Triple Sec** and is served with a lime wedge on the rim of a cocktail glass.

A similar but more trendy cocktail is simply known as a **Cranberry and Vodka** made in a highball glass filled with ice, 2 oz Vodka topped with cranberry juice.

The **Americano** is served in an a short, round, old-fashioned glass on ice. It is composed of 1/2 oz of **Campari** (20 -28% alcohol), 1/2 oz of **Sweet Vermouth**, topped with club soda and garnished with a twist of lemon and an orange slice. Popular in America since the 1900's, the Americano was invented in Italy in the 1860's.

From Mexico, the **Margarita** is made with 1 1/2oz **Tequila** (45 - 50% alcohol) oz 1/2 orange-flavored liqueur (**Triple Sec or Contreau**), and a dash of fresh lime juice, shaken and poured with ice into a specialized, stemmed, Margarita glass (or "straight up" without ice in an 8 oz highball glass) with salt on the rim, garnished with a lime wedge.

A **Rum and Coke** is made with 2 oz **Rum** (45% alcohol) and 4-6 oz cola beverage, served in a tall, highball glass over ice with a lime wedge.

The **Mimosa** is an excellent luncheon or brunch cocktail made with 3 1/2 oz chilled **Champagne**, 1-1/2 oz fresh orange juice and 1/2 oz **Triple Sec**, served in a champagne flute.

The **Screwdriver**, also popular at breakfast or brunch is made by mixing 1-1/2 oz Vodka (50% alcohol) with 6 oz orange juice and served over ice in an old-fashioned glass.

A **Bloody Mary** is made with 3 oz Tomato juice, 1 1/2 oz **Vodka** (50% alcohol), 1/2 oz Lemon juice, and 1 dash Worcestershire sauce, ground pepper and hot pepper sauce to taste, a celery stalk in a highball glass with a wedge of lemon or lime for garnish. It is traditionally thought to be a hangover cure.

The following, heavier cocktails made with whiskey may be more popular as a warming drink in Fall and Winter:

The classic **Manhattan** contains 2 oz of **Rye Whiskey** (37% alcohol), 1/2 oz Sweet Vermouth and Angostura bitters to taste (2 - 4 dashes). Stirred and strained into a chilled cocktail stem with a single cherry garnish.

A **'Perfect' Manhattan** has 2 oz of **Rye Whiskey** (37% alcohol), equal parts of Sweet and Dry Vermouth and is garnished with a lemon twist, shaken with ice and strained into a chilled cocktail glass.

The **Rob Roy** in honor of Scottish folk hero, Robert Roy McGreggor, also known as the Scotch Manhattan is mixed the same but substitute **Scotch**

Whiskey (40 - 50% alcohol) and omit the bitters, pour ice and all, into an stout, broad rimmed, old fashioned glass.

Classic After Dinner Drinks

Irish Coffee is made by adding 1 oz. Irish whiskey (40 - 50% alcohol) to one cup of coffee or espresso in a glass beaker or mug topped with heavy whipped cream.

Brandy, (45% alcohol) served by the ounce to taste in a short stemmed, snifter and warmed with the palm of your hand.

(If you are planning to have a dinner party at home for more than a few people, I recommend that you hire a professional bar tender to serve you and your guests. You will be the host with the most, and you will enjoy yourself more especially if you are also greeting, cooking and serving.)

To reiterate: sample the appetizers and savor one cocktail, before dinner drink or aperitif while the night is young. After that, again, a wise plan is to have no more than one adult beverage per hour throughout the evening or average even less than one drink per hour. After that, if you don't pace yourself intelligently, the results are predictable…

Intoxication

Drink 1 makes us tingle,
Drink 2 want to mingle,
Drink 3 losing faculties.
Drink 4 still surviving,
But we won't be driving,
Drink 5, Coffee, please?

Appetizers and Hors d'oeuvres

These tasty little finger foods are often helpfully high in fats and proteins. These ingredients accomplish two purposes: They take the edge off your appetite and can absorb alcohol in your stomach thereby slowing its effects. These are very good things if you want to keep your competitive edge, be your most charming, sophisticated self and be able to make good conversation through all five or seven courses of dinner plus two wine services and a champagne toast! The following are classic appetizer recipes you might sample at a cocktail party or serve at a party of your own:

Caviar Serve 1/2 tsp of black caviar on dollops of sour cream atop tiny, boiled, red potatoes, cut in half and scooped out, or firm crackers.

Rumaki Marinate in the refrigerator for 2 hours: 12 oz fresh chicken livers and one, 4oz can of water chestnuts in a simple savory sauce: 1 1/2 cups teriyaki sauce, 1/2 tsp minced garlic, 1/2 tsp minced fresh ginger root. Cut 12 slices of bacon in half. Wrap each half slice of bacon around one chicken liver half and a slice of water chestnut. Skewer with toothpicks. Bake in the oven on 350 until crispy. Drain on paper towels and serve cool.

Develed Eggs Peel and cut six, hard-boiled eggs in half, length-wise and remove the yolks. In a mixing bowl blend yolks, 1/4 cup mayonnaise, 1 tsp Dijon mustard, and 1 tsp apple cider vinegar. Stuff the egg white halves with the yolk mixture. Garnish with paprika . Serve cold.

1/2 inch cubes of the finest cheese with a toothpick in each one.

Fresh, Deveined Shrimp with Cocktail Sauce served on a bed of ice.

Art and Music

Knowing what you like in art and music helps you to define who you are and makes you a more interesting conversationalist. We surround ourselves with art and music. Sounds and images are refreshed daily with new, intimate, immediate and interactive forms of self expression. For the connoisseur of art and music, this lesson will give you a broad overview of man's image of himself as expressed in the evolution of art.

In the vast array of art through time, let us consider nine works of art, inventions or events chosen from highlights in the history of mankind. This exercise will help us feel continuity of human experience, brilliance of human expression and undeniable oneness of human life. These works represent man's image of himself. You may already know this, If not, look on-line for the items listed below. Note contemporary music of each age.

Man's Image of Himself

1.) Pre-historic Cave Paintings, Paleolithic Age, 32-10,000 BCE, drums
2.) Ancient Egyptian hieroglyphics, 1300 BCE, Music: flute, strings
3.) Ancient Greek pottery, 515 BCE, Music: drums, flutes, strings
4.) Chinese Terra Cotta Warrior Statues, 210 BCE, Music: flute, drums
5.) Mona Lisa, 1505 CE, Renaissance, harpsichord, strings, chants
6.) Telephone, 1847 carries voices long distances, Music: orchestras
7.) Automobile, 1894 transports passengers, Music: phonograph
8.) IBM 610 Auto-Point, Personal Computer, 1957, Rock 'n Roll, 45's
9.) Moon Landing, Apollo 11, 1961, Music: jazz, transistor radios, TV
10.) iPhone, 2007, music: Hip Hop, CDs, DVDs

Modern Art

The following is an overview of Modern Art for the Connoisseur. This lesson offers a quick look at the history of art as a background for the modern conversationalist and consumer of contemporary art. In the nineteenth and twentieth-centuries, oil painting re-emerged as a major form of artistic expression. Unlike photo-realism artists of the Renaissance, this time painters ushered in the evolution of man to the information age with expressions of human perception and cognition. It is helpful to have the following, basic knowledge of some of their individual contributions to our present vocabulary of visual imagery.

Modernism, 1850 - 1960's. A series of experimental trends in the arts initially striving for heightened Realism, includes Impressionism see Monet, Van Gogh and Degas, Klimt, Matisse, Mondrian and Kandinsky. Art Nouveau: see Louis Comfort Tiffany, Abstract Art: see Jackson Pollack, Pop (popular culture) Art, see Andy Warhol, Surrealism see Salvatore Dali, Cubism, see Picasso and Braque, Primitivism, see Paul Gauguin.

Post World War Two, the "Jazz Age" ushered in the International styles of Art Deco, Futurism and the Bauhaus, see Frank Lloyd Wright.

In the beginning decades of the twenty-first century, now engaged in the Digital Age follow giant advancements in personal computers, commercial satellites, transportation and cell phone technologies, we seem to be evolving toward one constant, connected culture on planet Earth.

Lesson Ten - Connoisseur - Activity - Study Menus

Study restaurant menus and practice pairing meals with appropriate beverages. Try cooking the international foods you enjoy. Educate your pallet.

Lesson Ten - Connoisseur - Essay

On the following blank page, write a 250 word essay about what you like in art and music.

Lesson Eleven

FORMAL ATTIRE

I JUST WANT to compliment your on how you both presented and conducted yourselves at the dining table. Bravo!

Thank you! Thank you for inviting us . And by the way, the food was delicious! The following are some helpful hints and guidelines for what is customarily worn at formal affairs. Formal attire is unique in that it is primarily uniform. Match the information below to 'Attire' notes found in the lower right corner of invitations. Consult with other guests or your hostess regarding modern trends in classic formal wear. Confirm that your personal choices meet standards of the event.

Black tie: (Evening events, after six p.m.) For Jill, this means a chic, beaded dress or high fashion, evening dress of fine fabric. A little black dress can be worn with proper accessorizing. **White Tie** For ladies, means a long formal gown with complimentary wrap and perhaps with matching shoes, long white gloves, tiaras, and a tiny evening bag.

Some evening bags have a hidden strap so that they can be hung on the back of your chair or over the shoulder and even brought to the dance floor. Larger bags should be placed under your chair, not on top of the table.

For Jack, **Black tie** means exactly that. Black Dinner Jacket, or Tuxedo, dress slacks and Black bow tie, or straight tie, with proper white dress shirt or tuxedo shirt, a black cummerbund or wide, pleated sash, shirt studs and cuff links (gold, silver, mother-of-pearl, or onyx) and appropriate shoes, they may be laced or slip-on preferably of the highest quality patent leather.

For a **White tie** affair, gentlemen wear a Black Tail Coat (having the front cut away so that the back is longer) with white shirt, tie and white waistcoat (vest) a cummerbund is not acceptable to wear with a tailcoat. White gloves and top hats may be worn, inquire in advance just how formal the event is. Occasionally, gentlemen and ladies may wear white gloves for dancing. Tuxedo shirts, jackets and dress shoes in any size can be rented.

Gentlemen sometimes wear white dinner jackets with bow ties and black slacks to dinner or cocktail parties, where ladies wear cocktail dresses.

Morning Suit: Daytime formal wear for men also known as lounge suit, is a gray or black coat with "tails" worn with a gray top hat, pale colored shirt, light colored tie, cream colored linen, silk or brocade waistcoat (vest) and pin-striped trousers, black or gray, lace-up leather shoes and possibly gray gloves.

Morning Dress: for Jill, means an elegant suit or dress with sleeves or a jacket, appropriate for the season and the weather; perhaps a hat could be worn and gloves if the event is very formal. Shoes should be chosen for indoors or for outside depending if the event is to be held in a garden or on grass, in a tent.

Jack, I suggest that you keep at least two business suits and a Navy Blue jacket or blazer to wear with a dress shirt, gray or tan slacks and tie. Wear black shoes with grey slacks and brown shoes with tan slacks. Learn to tie the most popular and well-known knot, the "Windsor knot." worn by gentlemen all over the world since its introduction by the Duke of Windsor in 1936. They say that learning to produce a well-tied knot is one of the first serious steps in a man's life.

The Long and the Short of a Windsor Knot

Practice makes perfect. Looking in the mirror, bring the tie over your head, lay the two ends on your chest making the thinner side approximately a third longer. Wrap the thin side around the wider side twice tucking its end between the two wraps and behind the tie's front panel. Pull the end down to fit, keeping the front of the tie approximately at the belt line. Adjust the knot for ideal, triangle shape and comfort.

Hair: Cascading layers of mid-length, healthy hair is in fashion now, but at formal affairs a young lady's hair can also be styled, and done-up, off the shoulders. For gentlemen it should be neat, trimmed and off the collar.

Teeth: Should be clean, white and sparkling. Diligent cleaning and checking in the mirror will pay off if you want others to feel comfortable close to you.

Nails: Fingernails should be kept neatly trimmed, filed and manicured. Ladies with open-toe shoes or strappy sandals will need pedicures too.

Shoes: When attending a banquet where there will be dancing, Jack's shoes should be lightweight, leather and made for dancing. At formal affairs, shoes should be black, dress or patent leather shoes with leather soles. Jill's dancing shoes should have high heels, with ankle straps for added support. For the desired effect of being 'light on her feet', she should be able to lift herself up on the balls of her feet, change or remove shoes while dancing.

Jewelry: Less is more where jewelry is concerned for the formal affair. One ring on each hand, for example. Now is the time to wear your diamonds, birthstones or any real gemstones, onyx and pearls, precious or semi-precious stones and tiaras.

To look your best, conform to tradition while showing an updated awareness of what is appropriate for you personally and for the occasion.

Lesson Eleven - Formal Attire - Activity - Personal Wardrobe Inventory

Take inventory of your personal wardrobe. You should have work clothes and shoes ready for five or six consecutive work days. For the occasional formal affair, keep a tuxedo or a little black dress and dress shoes on hand. Update your supply of appropriate casual clothes for different activities like work outs, house cleaning, sleeping and sports. Take pride in your appearance at all times, weed out worn-out, faded and dated items. Make regular charitable donations and sell pricey items.

Lesson Eleven - Formal Attire - Quiz

1. What is a 'black tie" event? _____.

2. Describe a 'black tie' uniform for men. _____
_____
_____.

3. What term is used for the sash worn with a tuxedo? _____
_____.

4. What does 'black tie' mean in ladies attire? _____
_____
_____.

5. What is a morning suit? _____
_____
_____.

6. What is a waist coat? _____
_____.

7. What is morning wear for ladies? _____
_____
_____
_____

8. What color slacks and shoes go with a navy blue blazer? _____
_____.

9. When should a lady not wear high heels? _____
_____.

10. What is the most popular knot? _____.

LESSON TWELVE

MOON LAKE

by TK Reilly
a 3-act play

Introduction

THIS IS YOUR opportunity to add a multi-cultural experience to your already impressive array of business skills. Here, as you step into the role of host in a billion dollar business transaction, you will negotiate the sale of a lifetime. Simply read the following script.

First, some reminders and tips: every executive knows that with any business meeting or presentation in any language, the two keys to success are research and preparation. This goes double for multi-lingual meetings.

1.) Know your product. Do your homework; stay alert, do not underestimate your customer and be well prepared with visual aids appropriate for the sale you seek to close. Ask intelligent questions about the customer's needs and be ready to match them to your product. Become familiar with several financing options. Know your product strengths and emphasize them. Be prepared to explain, long term benefits such as insurance and warranty details.

2.) Know your customer. Choose a venue for the lunch that will please by asking preferences in advance, offer to send a car or cars for your guest and his or her translator. Arrange to have your own translator attend the meeting. To celebrate the completion of a successful transaction, bring gifts for the buyer and members of the buyer's party. Know the menu of the venue in advance and try to learn what your guest prefers to have for lunch, at least take the time to educate yourself with a variety of suggested choices and matched beverages.

Know where the Exits, Restrooms and Bar are located in the venue and be sure to cover the cost of parking if your guests drive themselves to the meeting. If the meeting was your idea, you pay the bill and add a tip of at least 15%. Make sure that you arrive on time. In fact, not just on time, arrive early. If you are early, you are on time for you have allowed yourself time to properly join the company of others; to say hello, find your seat, hang up your over coat, get a beverage, etc. If you are just on time, you are late; and being late is not acceptable behavior, especially as a chronic habit because you are disrupting those who have already arrived and settled-in.

If you have called the meeting, visualize yourself taking command of the situation. Before departing to the meeting, go over your personal appearance check list adding specific body language, vocabulary and materials required. Practice protocol for the local bow, air kiss, handshake and presentation of business cards as appropriate for the country you are in. Your trustworthiness and salesmanship will be judged along with your comportment, professional readiness, pronunciation and even your scent. Be prepared for your personal best presentation. This means that you must appear confident, clean, well groomed, rehearsed and business-minded. Have that suit cleaned and pressed.

Any business meeting can be an oasis of civility and progress where executives move forward and close deals. This one can be so much more; it can assist you with passage from a weak economy and poor prospects through cultural boundaries into new territory. This play puts you where the buyers are.

Jack and Jill, please join me in the third act of Moon Lake and thank you for the inspiration, participation and for your assistance throughout Behave!

You are certainly welcome, we will see you at Moon Lake!

(Note: This is a business etiquette and protocol lesson and workshop activity. Moon Lake Development, BRICS Corporation, all the characters and terms of their contract are fictional. Lesson Twelve is an activity in itself, suggesting applications of all previous lessons in this book.

Moon Lake

by TK Reilly

Role 1.) **Mr. Seller, American Chief Executive Officer, Moon Lake Development** with business card, presentation, gifts, smart phone, pen and contract)

Role 2.) Mr. **Buyer, Chief Financial Officer, BRICS Corporation Executive Fund** (with business cards, and smart phone)

Role 3.) **Seller's translator**(with smart phone) translates during first two Acts, third Act is all English

Role 4.) **Buyer's translator** (with smart phone) translates during first two Acts, third Act is all English

Role 5.) **Mr. President, BRICS Corporation**

Role 6.) **Assistant to the President**

Narrator: Describes action

Chorus: Chants etiquette tips at timely intervals

Act I: Singapore Hotel

<u>Narrator</u>: Mr. Seller believes in the Moon Lake project in Central Florida. It is his family business. He arrived in Singapore yesterday, got a good night's sleep and continues to rehearse and plan for today's meeting. After several emails, telephone calls, and conference calls, today is the first time he will be meeting his customer in person. Convinced that they are very close to signing, Mr. Seller has flown to Singapore from Orlando for this meeting. He and his translator have practiced coordinating their sales presentation many times. As the curtain opens, Mr. Seller is on the phone to the Hotel Concierge.

<u>Mr. Seller</u>: *"Hello. This is Mr. Seller in room 207 calling to confirm reservations for my business meeting today at 2:00PM. Yes, there will be four of us and I requested a private room with AV equipment and a window. I believe my assistant has set up our sales model there already. Okay, I'll be right down to see it. Thank you."*

<u>Narrator</u>: Mr. Seller will rely on his expert translator who works in Portuguese, Russian, English and Chinese, all of the BRICS languages. He does not want to take a chance on offending with the wrong word or phrase. He hasbeen with Moon Lake Development since he graduated three years ago with an MBA from Harvard. They are presenting Phase One of the Moon Lake Development. After five years of planning, the time has come to market it. Phase One will become vacation homes for 300 BRICS Corporation executives.

The BRICS Corporation Executive Fund represents buyers from China, Brazil, India, Russia and South Africa who responded with interest to a marketing campaign targeting them over the past several months. Moon Lake Development is a good match for their needs. Today has been preceded by multiple business meetings of sales, finance and legal teams. This should be an easy closing but nothing will be left to chance. Today, the principals meet for the first time to discuss details of a sales contract.

Mr. Seller stands to practice speaking to the mirror once more before leaving the room. His business cards are printed on both sides; English on one side and the customer's language on the other. When presenting his business card (after a slight bow because he is in Asia) he will take it from his inside jacket pocket (near his heart) hold it forth with both hands and say in English,

Mr. Seller: *"Hello Mr. Buyer, I am Mr. Seller, here is my business card. This is my translator."*

Narrator: The Buyer, who is in another room in the same hotel, prepares for the same meeting. The Buyer practices greeting Mr. Seller with slight bow and offering his business card for exchange, says,

Mr. Buyer: *"Hello Mr. Seller, I am Mr. Buyer, and this is my translator. We represent the BRICS Corporation. Thank you for traveling so far to meet with us."*

Narrator: Suddenly Mr. Buyer's room phone rings. It is his translator calling to say that he will meet Mr. Buyer in the Hotel lobby in 20 minutes. Mr. Buyer agrees and proceeds to get ready. He ties an Windsor knot in his tie, puts on the silver cuff links his wife gave him for their 25th wedding anniversary, ties his shoes, puts on his suit jacket and gets to the elevator with time to spare. Mr. Buyer and his family speak English quite well conversationally and they observe many Western traditions. However he always brings his translator to international business meetings.

Narrator: Meanwhile, Mr. Seller greets his translator when he gets out of the elevator in the lobby. They walk together to the conference room to check arrangements for the meeting. the concierge leads them to a small meeting room with a harbor view. The room is equipped with a conference table with seating for six topped with carafes of water, coffee and tea, paper pads and pens. There is a large, flat screen TV on the wall above a side table with USB ports. They start the Moon Lake video presentation, check the room temperature and place Moon Lake Development annual reports at each place on the table.

Mr. Seller and his translator then walk to the lobby and are waiting there when Mr. Buyer and his translator arrive. They all meet at the appointed time.

Narrator: Of course the first order of business is Protocol, introductions and the exchange of business cards.

Chorus: **Protocol**

Success Begins with Social Graces,

Put it There, with the Names and Faces,

an Air-Kiss-Hug in many Places!

You'll Make a Good Impression Now,

Shake their hand, Hug, Air-Kiss, Bow!"

Make a Good Impression Now!

Narrator: Just as practiced, after a slight bow with eyes lowered, Mr. Seller extends his business card to Mr. Buyer (with the client's language facing out) he then extends his hand, for a firm handshake with eye contact. He gives not just one, but 5 business cards so that Mr. Buyer can in turn give a card to others in his group. In English, he says,

Seller: *"Hello Mr. Buyer, I am Mr. Seller, CEO of Moon Lake Development, here is my business card. This is my translator."*

Mr. Buyer responds as he had practiced earlier, *"Hello Mr. Seller, I am Mr. Buyer, and this is my translator. We represent the BRICS Corporation Executive Fund. Thank you for traveling so far to meet with us."*

Narrator: Mr. Seller, as the host, is the next to speak.

Mr. Seller: *"We have much to discuss, the conference room is this way. He walks backward to the elevator to show respect by not turning his back to his guest. The translators follow.*

Narrator: The foursome make their way to the conference room where a smiling hostess greets them saying, " Mr. Seller, Please come this way, your room is ready." The room has one long conference table and two side tables one in the back and one on the side opposite the windows. In the center of the conference table, sits a model of the Moon Lake Development. Mr. Seller indicates that two chairs facing the window are for Mr. Buyer and his translator. Mr. Seller sits across from Mr. Buyer and the translators sit facing each other. Everyone's smart phones are silenced and in their pockets to be checked for urgent messages every half hour or so.

Narrator: At the far end of the table on the wall, a large flat TV screen, displays a sunny video of Moon Lake's sparkling water. A light breeze is blowing through tall grass and trees along its shoreline.

Mr. Seller: Says to Mr. Buyer, *"Thank you so much for meeting with me today, I have much information to share with you. I'd like to start with the financial report."*

Mr. Buyer: answers, *"I agree, this is all very interesting. The video and the model must be of Moon Lake, it looks like a wonderful place, very inviting."*

Mr. Seller: responds, *"I am glad that you like the video, as they say, "A picture is worth a thousand words. Each of the 300 homes in Phase One has a view similar to this of Moon lake. This DVD shows sunrise, midday, sunset, moonrise and moonset in summer. The view we are seeing right now is midday in summer. As you know, Florida winters are mild and the lake is beautiful then too. "*

Narrator: Mr. Seller picks up the annual report in front of him, opens it and continues:

Mr. Seller: *"For more information regarding the climate there, please see the environment chapter in the back of the annual report. But first, I want to draw your attention to the company's earnings, especially over the past five years. We have enjoyed solid growth, even during economic downturns."*

Narrator: Mr. Buyer and his translator open the annual reports in front of them to follow the financial details of Mr. Seller's presentation.

Mr. Seller: *"The land was purchased during real estate boom times in the 1980's with investment capital from our parent company, Insurance United Fund. Moon Lake Development investment account grew rapidly. By 2001, Moon Lake Championship Golf Course and Country Club were built and our engineers were excavating and moving earth, creating a man-made second lake, the smaller, Lotus Lake and the fishing stream that connects them. By 2006, plans for the Shopping Village and Phase One of Moon Lake Housing were ready to go. At that time, market research told us to seek buyers from stronger economies like the BRICS Corporation Fund. Moon Lake Phase One, vacation homes are ideal, International, executive investment properties."*

Narrator: **Mr. Seller pours ice water for Mr. Buyer and himself and takes a sip.**

Mr. Buyer asks, *"What is on the property now? How much of your plan has been developed?"*

Mr. Seller: *"The Golf Course and Country Club are fully developed, along with the tennis courts and exercise facility. the Club House has 150 hotel rooms for golfing tournament players and guests. As you know, golf is very popular in Florida and the location of the property makes it attractive for celebrity competitions. Revenues from the golf industry have made the property a good investment for the Insurance United Fund. As you can see in the report these have been profitable. Moon Lake Shopping village and Culture Center are nearly finished now too.*

Narrator: **Mr. Buyer consults with his translator who then asks,**

Translator: *" I see that Moon Lake has been a good investment for owners of the Insurance United Fund, will they also share in ownership of the homes of Moon Lake Phase One?"*

Mr. Seller: *"Good question, and the answer is No, because Moon Lake and Insurance United are two completely separate entities. However, they share a symbiotic relationship. Country Club memberships and golfing privileges are included with the purchase price of all of Moon Lake's home sites. All the homeowners share in the cooperative ownership of Moon Lake Phase One as a group or community. This is a variation of the concept of condominium ownership."*

Mr. Buyer asks, *"The benefits of investment housing ownership seem truly excellent. What are the responsibilities that come with ownership? Are there additional costs?*

Mr. Seller: *"No, owner's monthly mortgage payments include common area maintenance fees for landscaping, refuse removal and street lighting and these* are all regularly scheduled. There are optional upgrades to Country Club membership and the Performing Arts Association but those are arranged by choice individually."

Narrator: **Mr. Buyer consults with his translator who then asks,**

Translator: *"Mr. Seller, please explain the Country Club upgrades and the Performing Arts Association membership?"*

Mr. Seller: "Certainly, with home ownership, you receive an Executive Golf Club membership entitling you to one free round of golf per week on the 18-hole Executive Course, plus use of the putting green, chipping green, practice bunker and locker room. the executive Club membership also includes a Social Membership with charging privileges in the Country Club Dining Room, Bar and Snack Bar. For an additional annual fee, you can always upgrade to a Championship Course membership which offers priority tee times on a more challenging course with professional training and celebrity encounters.

Our market research showed that people who travel and own properties tend to like a mix of sports and the arts. So to balance the golf lifestyle, we created the Performing Arts Association. Members can purchase season tickets at a discount. World Class entertainers and Shows will be scheduled in the Moon Lake Culture Center and *concerts will be scheduled in the Plum Tree Park open air Arena."*

Mr. Buyer: *"Mr. Seller, As you know, BRICS Corporation Fund represents executives who are ready to invest in vacation homes in Florida. What is the price to reserve a home in Phase One of Moon Lake Village? "*

Mr. Seller: responds, *"Reservations for each of the home sites are $10,000 minimum. The homes themselves are offered in three price ranges. The deposit or down-payment will be held in escrow while transactions are finalized. The more expensive homes will require additional deposits at closing.*

Narrator: **Mr. Buyer asks his translator to ask the next question,**

Mr. Buyer's translator: *"One more question, Does ownership require US citizenship?"*

Narrator: *Mr. Seller answers the question,*

Mr. Seller: *"Citizenship is not a requirement for ownership it is an added benefit. Moon Lake's international marketing plan is based on a mutually beneficial clause in US Immigration law, known as EB - 6, providing Green Cards to* foreign investors who pay $500,000 for the purchase of real estate properties which in turn bring financing for the creation of jobs in rural America. By satisfying the terms of this clause, we can move forward offering foreign investors added benefits of citizenship while creating long term benefits for Floridians."

Narrator: Mr. Buyer consults with his translator who says,

Mr. Buyer's translator: "We would like a moment to consult with our home office."

Narrator: Mr. Seller stands and suggests they all take a 15 minute break. This will give everyone a moment to check messages talk with associates and visit the restrooms. He invites his guests to take a closer look at the Moon Lake Development model when they return, he will tell them more of the history of the project, explain more financial details and discuss building options and features and answer more questions.

He senses that the BRICS Corporation will move ahead with the purchase.

end of the First Act

Narrator: The video on the wall behind the model catches everyone's eye. We pause to watch as the blue sky blushes into evening, golden flashes of sunset sparkle on the water's surface and a warm glow paints the pines along the shore of Moon Lake.

Act II: Sunset

Narrator: When we return, two people have joined the group, the esteemed, Mr. President, of the BRICS Corporation Fund, and his assistant. We find Mr. Seller standing beside the model with his guests.

Mr. Seller: "Well, first let me say, it is a great honor to have you join us, Mr. President. Thank you for coming. To give a tangible, overview showing the scope and size of the Moon Lake Village property, we brought this three-dimensional, scale model. With this you can identify exactly which lots you wish to purchase. As you know, Moon Lake the larger, upper lake is a natural lake. Beginning In 2006, our engineers added the golf course, the lower lake, and the connecting stream."

Mr. Buyer: asks, *"Where exactly will Phase One be built?"*

Mr. Seller: using a pointer, says " This area here, is Phase One. It includes the Shopping Village, Plum Tree Park and the 300 home sites around Moon Lake. Phase Two, one hundred home sites, will be built along the fishing stream on the opposite bank from the Golf Courses. Phase Three will be 100 homes around the lower lake, known as Lotus Lake, where the waterfall, gazebo and Neighborhood Gardens will be."

Mr. Buyer: asks, *"Will there be restaurants in the shopping village? What shops will be there?"*

Mr. Seller: continues, *"Moon Lake Shopping Village is located here. It will offer amenities to support the needs of the residents and the community. The Village shops will include a pet shop, garden shop, clothing and jewelry boutique, full service salon, grocery store, bakery, restaurants, coffee shop and a boating and fishing store. We have also provided urgent care facilities, maid service and care giving agencies, a travel agency, a full-service gas station, a drug store and a bank. All the service managers are multi-lingual. There is a beach and a marina on the lake side and a pool and tennis courts on the opposite side of the Country Club which itself has 150 rooms for visitors, a Culture Center and an Art Gallery.*

Mr. Buyer responds: " *Will the homes all look alike? Please explain how residents choose if they are interested in different sized homes with different floor plans at different prices?"*

Mr. Seller: *"We offer three different, but visually compatible home designs to choose from. They are all natural wood homes with stone foundations, fireplaces, wood floors and cabinets in your choice of two, three or four bedrooms. The homes are matched with various decks, porches, garages, kitchen designs and number of bedrooms, within the range of 2,500 square feet at the beginning price of $500,000 to 3,500 square feet, priced up to $800,000. Our architects and builders can begin work on site selections and home designs immediately."*

Mr. Buyer: speaks, *"Many of our executives look forward to staying in Florida and playing golf during winter months. Are residents allowed to fish in the lakes and the fly-fishing stream? Please describe the Neighborhood Gardens. What is grown there? "*

Mr. Seller: *"Home ownership gives access and full use of all the amenities Moon Lake has to offer including golfing, club house and fishing privileges everywhere for one's own use. For those who enjoy gardening, owners may reserve a ten by twenty foot plot of land and a small potting shed in the Neighborhood*

Gardens, for growing vegetables, fruits and flowers, also for the home owners private enjoyment."

Narrator: Following Mr. Seller's lead, everyone is seated to continue discussions. Mr. President is now seated across from Mr. Seller and his assistant is seated across from Mr. Seller's translator.

Mr. Seller: asks Mr. President. *"What do you think of Moon Lake so far? As you may have read in our annual report, we have two other developments in North America, this is the first one we have marketed Internationally. Our other developments are located in Tennessee and Nevada and are fully occupied. The central Florida location is unique because it has the golf course, is close to Disney World in Orlando, cruise ships in Miami, Sports events and entertainment in Tampa and it is located near two international airports. It is already fully functioning within a multi-cultural community and enjoys all the benefits of central Florida's tourism market."*

Mr. President: responds, *" It seems you have thought of everything. We at BRICS Corporation value your commitment and see the potential in your Florida development. You have brought Disney-style destination design and quality executive vacation homes together with many added benefits of the coveted green card. What is the price to reserve all 300 homes, the entire Phase One of Moon Lake Village? "*

Mr. Seller: answers, *"To reserve the entire Phase One requires a deposit of $3,000,000 today.*

Mr. President: says, *"I am authorized to arrange a transfer of the required deposit today. My team, working with your architects and designers, can act as liaison for all buyers in the plan. We will also arrange consultations for each buyer, to select individual home design preferences. "*

Mr. Seller: responds, *"I have the contract ready for your signature."*

Mr. President: says," *I will sign the contract!"*

Narrator: During the signing of the contract, champagne glasses and chilled bottles are brought in. Mr. Seller and Mr. President both stand, they shake hands and smile. Mr. Seller raises his champagne glass and speaks,

Mr. Seller: *" This calls for a celebration! " I would like to propose a toast!"*

Narrator: "POP" After opening the champagne bottle, a waiter steps forward and pours champagne, first for Mr. Seller and Mr. President, then the others. Everyone raises their glasses.

Mr. Seller: continues, *"It is a great pleasure doing business with you. Our next meeting will be a formal dinner in Florida, after the ground breaking ceremony for BRICS Corporation's new, vacation home site, Moon Lake Village, Phase One!"*

Narrator: Everyone drinks champagne and applauds the great success of their negotiations.

In the video on the wall behind them, brilliant hues of lavender blend into indigo and an iridescent full moon ascends the sky over Moon Lake.

Intermission

Act III: Moonrise

Narrator: Three months later, fifty top BRICS Corporation executives and their spouses arrive in Florida for a gala celebration and the ground breaking ceremony. The celebration banquet will held in the 'Watercolors' dining room, where decor is inspired by jungle and tropical forest art of Post-Impressionists, Gauguin and Rousseau. Moon Lake Country Club's Chef Nathan, has chilled the Vicheyssoise (potato soup), ordered the finest freshLobster for the Fish Course - the 2nd Course, and Filet Mignon for the Meat Course - the 4th Course. The dining room Sommelier (wine steward) has paired them with rare wines. The white will be chilled and the red decanted (uncorked) and allowed to breathe' and both will be served at the appropriate times as will champagne. There will be ice water with lemon and baskets of bread set on each table. The steaks will be broiled to medium-rare perfection, served with bite-sized, baked potatoes and the lobster tails will be served atop pre- cracked shells with asparagus spears with hollandaise, The 5th course (Salad) will consist of field greens, featuring arugula with pine nuts, raspberry-vinaigrette dressing. Dessert, (6th course) offers a choice of baked Alaska or Cherries Jubilee. Coffee, the 7th course is served with nuts, thus the reference to Seven - Course dinners as having, "Soup to Nuts"

Behave!

Narrator: Standing, smiling, Mr. Seller surveys the full dining room from on stage, he steps up to the podium. Greeted by applause, he raises his hands and says,

Mr. Seller: *" Thank you, thank you, everyone. Welcome, welcome and thank you for coming. Mr. President, let me personally thank you for bringing vision and good fortune together, making tonight's celebration possible, please join me at the podium.*

Narrator: Mr. President gets up from the table and walks to the podium. The two gentlemen greet one another, smile, bow slightly, shake hands and hug, then they turn toward the audience and several cameras flash. Mr. President speaks,

Mr. President: *" Thank you Mr. Seller, it is an honor to make history here with you at the ground breaking ceremony for Moon Lake, Phase One. We appreciate the community you have created here in Florida and your Southern Hospitality. Tonight, I speak for all of the BRICS Corporation executives who look forward to enjoying their vacation homes here, in saying, Thank you!"*

Mr. Seller: *" Thank you. Now in honor of your presence and investment in America, please stand as the band plays the introduction to each our national anthems and the color guard brings each of our national flags into the room for display."*

Narrator: Everyone stands and applauds continuously as the band plays and a color guard marches into the room with the flags and place them in stands upon the stage. Few people sing due to strict national codes of conduct, but everyone enthusiastically applauds the international gesture. Beginning with the "Star Spangled Banner" and the red, white and blue flag of the United States of America, also known as, 'Old Glory,' then Brazil's national anthem, "Hino Nacional Brazilerio" and brilliant, green flag, followed by the "National Anthem of the Russian Federation, and it's white, blue and red striped flag, then India's anthem, "Jana, Gana, Mana" with its orange white and green striped flag, the "National Anthem of the Republic of China," with China's brilliant red flag and South Africa's distinctive, six-colored flag of unity and combined anthem, "The Call of South Africa."

After the procession, Mr. Seller invites everyone to be seated and enjoy the banquet and entertainment. (There are programs on the tables.) He finds his seat at table #1. Automatically, when he first sits down, he remembers his etiquette training and checks the six items in his place setting before the meal.

<u>Chorus:</u> **Place Setting Rhyme**

    Hey, Diddle Diddle,

    My Plate in the Middle

    And we'll be eating soon.

    My Fork on the Left

    Below my Bread Plate

    Across from My Cup and Spoon

    My Knife on the Right

    Its Blade facing in

    And now we can begin.

Narrator: He then sits and picks up his napkin and places it on his lap. He takes a piece of Foccacia bread from a serving basket on the table, places the bread on his bread plate (at his left) and passes the basket to Mr. Buyer who is seated on his right. Mr. Seller then breaks off a bite-sized piece of bread, dips it into the dipping oil on the bread plate and pops it into his mouth. Others at the table follow his lead, deploying their napkins and breaking bread.

<u>Chorus:</u> "Mabel, Mabel, if you're able, Keep your elbows off the table!"

Narrator: After swallowing the bread, (lest he is caught speaking with food in his mouth) Mr. Seller cleans his finger tips on his napkin and takes a sip of water from the goblet at his right. He resists the urge to put his elbows on the table as he might at home but he does lean forward slightly as he speaks.

Narrator: He has just told Mrs. Seller, sitting on his left, "You look beautiful tonight," when, as expected, the soup course arrives. Remembering the rhyme for sipping soup properly, Mr. and Mrs.

Behave!

Seller pick up their soup spoons (from above their chargers), take a sip and with that, everyone begins to dine.

<u>Chorus</u>: " Out to Sea and Back to Me! Sssiiiipp! Out to Sea and Back to Me! Sssiiiippp!

Out to Sea and Back to Me! Sssiiiippp! "

<u>Narrator</u>: The band is softly playing Latin rhythms, when a vocalist steps Into the spotlight and begins a Brazilian rumba. Three brightly dressed, exhibition dance couples sway through the room as she sings. The music then shifts gradually to strings, setting a classical mood.

<u>Narrator</u>: After the soup course is cleared, the white wine and (2nd Course -Fish) Lobster is served next. Although there are several courses, portions are small and therefore, not too filling. For most efficient use of the knife and fork, Mr. and Mrs. Seller use Continental Style of dining to slice and eat the Lobster, and then American Style to graze upon their vegetables. Combining both styles in this way is known as the Concert Style of dining. Soon, the white wine glasses are removed and the dishes are cleared. And the 3rd Course, a delicate, Lemon Sorbet to clear the pallet, is placed before them.

Suddenly, two ballerinas appear in spot lights, one at each end of the dining room. With them, needing no introduction, the familiar strains of Tchaikovsky's ,"Dance of the Sugar Plum Fairy" begins, these lovely girls represent Russia of course.

<u>Narrator</u>: Red wine is poured for and the 4th Course, Filet Mignon (or a substitute vegetarian dish is served).

After the dishes are cleared and the wine glasses are removed, the 5th course, (Salad) is served. During the 5th course, a delightful troupe of dancers and musicians in traditional Indian costumes take the stage and perform the spirited "Cobra Dance."

As the applause begins to recede, everyone is alerted by the sound of chimes, a gong, and soon large drums pulled on a cart by men enters the room. Behind them, a Chinese Dragon weaves its way through the room bestowing everyone who feeds it, with good luck.

Finally, Champagne and Desserts are served. Mr. Seller stands, placing his napkin on the seat of his chair, he walks to the stage, and takes the microphone while a large frame is brought to the stage on an easel covered with a cloth. He says,

Mr. Seller: "*This has been a remarkable* evening. Before we go, I would like to make a presentation. Mr. President this original work of art was commissioned especially for you as a gift from the developers of Moon Lake Phase One."

Mr. Narrator: Mr. Seller removes the cloth to reveal a colorful landscape painting of the property. Mr. Buyer stands, and says,

Mr. Buyer: "*Thank you Mr. Seller, it is a very beautiful piece of art, a tribute to you and your company. I wish to give a gift to you as well."*

Mr. Narrator: Mr. Buyer's assistant brings a package to Mr. Seller on the stage.

Mr. Buyer: *adds, "This is a fountain pen make of South African gold!"*

Mr. Seller: *"Mr. President, thank you very much, I am honored to receive this excellent pen, I will treasure this always.*

And now, I thank you all for coming tonight. I know that many of us have early tee-times; but for those of you who wish to join me for after dinner drinks in the Casino on the riverboat," Moon Dance," we leave from the dock downstairs in 20 minutes for a moonlit ride around the lake." "Thank you again for coming."

Narrator: Later, we join Jack, Jill and TK on the riverboat observation deck to watch a majestic moon bounce along tree tops and dance lightly before us across the water aptly named, Moon Lake.

The End

Behave!

Lesson One - Inspiration - Quiz Answers:

1. About e thousand years ago. **2.** They used mathematics. **3.** Global Positioning Satellites. **4.** 1621 **5.** Forks, Fingers and Chop sticks. **6.** Courtesy. **7.** Declaration of Independence, Constitution and Bill of Rights. **8.** 1837 -1901. **9.** Theodore Roosevelt **10.** the Stock Market Crash of 1929 started the Great Depression which lasted until 1941 when America entered World War Two.

Lesson Two - Comportment - Quiz Answers:

1. to behave. **2.** Robert's Rules of Order. **3.** private club with good dinning and conference facilities. **4.** Personality test results can enhance our resume, show us our strengths and help us understand traits in others. **5.** online presence **6.** applied science. **7.** right foot. **8.** left foot. **9.** She has the rear view. **10.** He leads the dance by gently sending signals to her with the finger tips and palm of his right hand on her back.

Lesson Three - Protocol - Quiz - Answers:

1. the rules of meeting. **2.** The Handshake, Hug, Bow, Air-kiss and Curtsey, are physical protocol exchanged in meetings. **3.** Madam. **4.** remember titles and names. **5.** Short Term Memory (STM), lasts only about 20 seconds, and Long Term Memory (LTM), which can last a life time. **6.** Think of a fruit, vegetable or animal name that begins with the same letter. The person's name should come up later when you picture the fruit, vegetable or animal. **7.** Say the person's name when you are introduced, say it again while you are conversing with them and introduce them to someone else right away. **8.** The texture and color and embossing of your business card can cause tactile and visual memory links. **9.** Write the person's name with notes on your first impression of them. **10.** business cards, data bases, notes, photos.

Lesson Six - Dinner Conversation - Crossword Puzzle - Answers:

Down:
2. mild flattery = compliment
3. drop the ball = lapse
5. big grin = smile
7. anecdote = story
8. hostess gift = bouquet
11. melting pot = culture

Across:
1. non-confrontational = tactful
4. good listener = charmer
6. coward = bully
9. magic word = please
10. vulgar language = taboo

Lesson Seven - Correspondence - Quiz - Answers:

1. closure. **2.** to follow any gift, interview, reception or act of kindness **3.** within three days **4.** friendly greeting, name the actual gift, tell why you like it, additional comment, friendly closing, your first name in ink. **5. 6.** Actions **7.** Who, What, When Where. **8.** RSVP, Attire. **9.** two weeks **10.** three - five days.

Lesson Nine - The Concert Style - Quiz - Answer

A. at rest = X , **B.** finished = (\)

Lesson Eleven - Formal Attire - Quiz - Answers:

1. events held in the evening after six p.m. **2.** black dinner jacket and slacks, tuxedo shirt and black dress shoes. **3.** cummerbund **4.** little black dress, beaded evening dress, cocktail dress **5.** a grey coat with 'tails', grey top hat, pale dress shirt, waist coat, pinstripe trousers **6.** a tan or white brocade vest worn with a "tail coat" **7.** elegant suit or dress with sleeves or a jacket, perhaps a hat and gloves **8.** grey slacks/black shoes, tan slacks/brown shoes **9.** to a garden party or a reception held in a tent **10.** Windsor

Sources

http://donnayoung.org/penmanship/p09/smprint/copy/rules-civility.txt

www.reuters.com/news

www.erie.gov/stopdui/bac_calculator.asp
www.merriam-webster.com/dictionary/comport
http://news.nationalpost.com
/2011/03/25royal-wedding-etiquette-how-to-fit-in-with-the-royals
www.recipe.com, allrecipes.com, myrecipes.com

www.acs.org/undergrad, inChemistry, Upgrade Your Online Image

Author Biography

Teresa Kathryn Grisinger Reilly (TK) is an Art Historian and Instructional systems designer who lives in Florida on the Gulf of Mexico. She works in three languages and enjoys international travel. TK has trained hundreds of etiquette instructors and thousands of students in table manners, social protocol and ballroom dance. Her first book, titled, Etiquette Lessons, Girls & Boys at the Table, Teens at the Table, for K - 12, was published in 2004, Etiquette Lessons, Vol. II, Modern Manners, for teens and College students along with the Student Workbook, in 2007, and in 2012 she published, Behave! her third book of Etiquette Lessons, with Behave! Companion Workbook, for executive adults. For more information. please visit: www.etiquettelessons.com and like Etiquette Lessons Foundation on Facebook. Copyright 2011, 2012, Etiquette Lessons Foundation. All rights reserved.

Made in the USA
San Bernardino, CA
03 February 2013